A PHILOSOPHY FOR NEFA

A PHILOSOPHY FOR NEFA

VERRIER ELWIN

With a foreword

by

THE PRIME MINISTER OF INDIA

A Philosophy for N E FA

ISBN : 978-81-8205-491-2

Reprinted in 2009 in India by
Isha Books
B-63, 1st Floor
New Gupta Colony,
Near DDA Market,
Delhi - 110009
First Published in 1957

Printed at : Vishal Kaushik Printers, Delhi

I am alarmed when I see — not only in this country but in other great countries too — how anxious people are to shape others according to their own image or likeness, and to impose on them their particular way of living. We are welcome to our way of living, but why impose it on others? This applies equally to national and international fields. In fact, there would be more peace in the world if people were to desist from imposing their way of living on other people and countries.

I am not at all sure which is the better way of living, the tribal or our own. In some respects I am quite certain their's is better. Therefore, it is grossly presumptuous on our part to approach them with an air of superiority, to tell them how to behave or what to do and what not to do. There is no point in trying to make of them a second-rate copy of ourselves.

— JAWAHARLAL NEHRU

On the top of all this variety of nature and man in Africa there impinge western civilization and western industrialism. Will their impact level down the variety, reducing the proud diversity of tribes and races to a muddy mixture, their various cultures to a single inferior copy of our own? Or shall we be able to preserve the savour of difference, to fuse our culture and their's into an autochthonous civilization, to use local difference as the basis for a natural diversity of development?

— JULIAN HUXLEY

An open and flexible mind, which recognizes the need of transformation and faithfully sets itself to apprehend new conditions, is a prerequisite of man's usefulness. But those who take my point of view will try to bring all change into harmony with the fundamentals drawn from the past. If the past to a man is nothing but a dead hand, then in common honesty he must be an advocate of revolution. But if it is regarded as the matrix of present and future, whose potency takes many forms but is not diminished, then he will cherish it scrupulously and labour to read its lessons, and shun the heady short-cuts which end only in blank walls.

— LORD TWEEDSMUIR

CONTENTS

FOREWORD

Some four or five months ago, Dr Verrier Elwin sent me a typescript of this small book and suggested that I might write a foreword to it. It was easy enough to write a few lines, but I did not wish to do so before I had read the typescript. I would have been in any event interested in reading it as the challenge to us from the North-East Frontier Agency fascinates me. I was fully occupied with various activities at the time, and so I put this typescript aside for a leisure hour or two. That leisure did not come. A few days ago there was a gentle reminder from Verrier Elwin and I felt a little ashamed at having kept him waiting for all this time. And so, in spite of numerous other activities and engagements, including election work, I have read through this very interesting little book.

Verrier Elwin has done me the honour of saying that he is a missionary of my views on tribal affairs. As a matter of fact, I have learnt much from him, for he is both an expert on this subject with great experience and a friend of the tribal folk. I have little experience of tribal life and my own views, vague as they were, have developed under the impact of certain circumstances and of Verrier Elwin's own writings. It would, therefore, be more correct to say that I have learnt from him rather than that I have influenced him in any way.

I came across the tribal people first, rather distantly, in various parts of India other than the North-East Frontier. These tribes were the Gonds, the Santals and the Bhils. I was attracted to them and liked them and I had a feeling that we should help them to grow in their own way.

Later, I came in touch with the tribal people of the North-East Frontier of India, more especially of the Hill Districts of Assam. My liking for them grew and with it came respect. I had no sensation of superiority over them. My ideas were not clear at all, but I felt that we should avoid two extreme courses : one was to treat them as anthropological specimens for study and the other was to allow them to be engulfed by the masses of Indian humanity. These reactions were instinctive and not based on any knowledge or experience. Later, in considering various aspects of these problems and in discussing them with those who knew much more than I did, and more especially with Verrier Elwin, more definite ideas took shape in my mind and I began to doubt how far the normal idea of progress was beneficial for these people and, indeed, whether this was progress at all in any real sense of the word. It was true that they could not be left cut off from the world as they were. Political and economic forces impinged upon them and it was not possible or desirable to isolate them. Equally undesirable, it seemed to me, was to allow these forces to function freely and upset their whole life and culture, which had so much of good in them.

The reading of this book has clarified my mind and helped me to have more definite views on the subject. I agree not only with the broad philosophy and approach of Verrier Elwin, but with his specific proposals as to how we should deal with these fellow-countrymen of ours. I hope that our officers and others who have to work with the tribals of NEFA will read carefully what Dr Elwin has written and absorb this philosophy so that they may act in accordance with it. Indeed, I hope that this broad approach will be applied outside the NEFA also to other tribals in India.

I hope the reading of this book will not be confined to our officers, but that it will have a wider audience. Our people all over India should know more about this problem and should develop affection and respect for these fine people. Above all, I hope there will be no attempt made to impose other ways of life on them in a hurry. Let the changes come gradually and be worked out by the tribals themselves.

It is true that the isolated life that our officers live in some of these tribal areas is a strain on them. But they must remember that the problems they deal with are a challenge to us and that they are privileged to be engaged in this great adventure.

JAWAHARLAL NEHRU

New Delhi,
February 16, 1957

PREFACE

Some time ago Shri K. L. Mehta remarked to me: 'Unless we are clear in our minds about what we are trying to do, unless, in fact, we have a philosophy behind all our activities, we may do more harm than good with the money and labour we spend.' This remark has inspired me to write down what I conceive to be the 'philosophy' which inspires or should inspire what we are trying to do in the North-East Frontier Agency. In the last two years a good many directives on fundamental policy have been issued. What I have done here is to try to give some of the reasons behind these directives and to discuss them with the help of actual examples, and in a fuller and freer manner than would be possible in an official document. This booklet must not be taken as in any way a directive, nor as a series of official instructions. It is rather a personal approach to the problem, though I have put forward my own views within the main outlines of the accepted policy of the Administration.

I have called myself a missionary of the Prime Minister's gospel and it is from that point of view that I have approached the many problems facing us. I did not come to tribal India (now exactly twenty-five years ago) from a school of anthropology, but from Gandhiji's ashram at Sevagram. I have always, I am afraid, been a very bad 'Gandhi man', but I have never forgotten some of the lessons he taught me. One of these was that, in his own words, 'we must approach the poor with the mind of the poor' — so too we must approach the tribesman with the mind of the tribesman. Another was the importance of simplicity : I saw something of Gandhiji's work in the villages of Gujerat and how he based everything on the local economy, worked through local institutions, avoided luxurious and unnecessary innovations, and concentrated everything on a few fundamental and essential needs. And yet another lesson was the importance of the individual. The tribal folk are not 'specimens', 'types' or 'cases'; they are *people*; they are human beings exactly like ourselves in all fundamental ways. We are part of them and they are part of us; there is no difference. They live under special conditions; they have developed along certain special lines; they have their own outlook and ways of doing things. But the ultimate human needs, aspirations, loves and fears are exactly the same as our's.

With this background, I have tried to apply the Prime Minister's humane and scientific ideals to concrete situations. To do this loyally and intelligently is, I believe, the chief source of hope for the people of NEFA.

Shillong : August 29, 1956

VERRIER ELWIN

Part One

THE FUNDAMENTAL PROBLEM

As I see it, the fundamental problem before us is this : what, from their point of view, is the best thing for the people of NEFA?

Is there not a case for the view that by and large they will probably be happier if they are left alone, or at least very largely alone, in the grandeur and freedom of their hills? They lack many of the amenities of life, but on the other hand they are free : no one interferes with them; they are able to live according to their own religion and traditions. Voltaire's Candide, after exploring all the civilizations of his contemporary world, came to the final conclusion that there was no greater happiness than in cultivating one's own garden. Why not let them do so?

On the other hand, it may be argued, would it not be better to 'civilize' them as rapidly as possible? Their life is nasty, brutish and short; their art is crude, their religion a medley of superstitions; they are dirty and diseased. As Charles Dickens, in a curious 'reprinted piece' on the Noble Savage, once urged, it is highly desirable to civilize the 'howling, whistling, clucking, stamping, jumping, tearing savage' as soon as possible off the face of the earth.

Few of us today would adopt either of these views in their entirety, certainly not if they are expressed in so crude a form. Yet the two policies have both been advocated, and followed, in India during the past fifty years.

The Policy of 'Leave Them Alone'

The British Government inclined, on the whole, to leave the tribesmen alone, partly because the task of administration, especially in the wild border areas, was difficult and unrewarding, partly from a desire to quarantine the tribes from possible political infection, and partly because a number of officers sincerely held the view that the people were better and happier as they were.

There is nothing that is specifically British about this policy and it certainly has nothing to do with anthropology. It derives from the very old pastoral tradition of classical Europe, the *beatus vir* of Horace, the Hortulan Saint of Sarbiewski, the Noble Savage of Rousseau, which saw in the untutored peasant someone better than urban and sophisticated man. In modern times such writers as R. L. Stevenson, Pierre Loti, Hermann Melville and Gauguin have also pressed this view, and there is something to be said for it. In many ways the simple tribal has the advantage of us, and contact with civilization has, all over the world, impaired his fine qualities.

This policy is exposed to at least three important criticisms. In the first place it has rarely been implemented in practice. There are some twenty million tribal people in India, and before Independence little was done for them. At the same time, they were not in actual fact left alone. They were exploited by landlords and zamindars, robbed by money-lenders, cheated by merchants. While national social workers were forbidden to work among them, foreign missionaries were freely admitted to their territories with the result that many tribes lost their traditional cultures.

Secondly, the belief in the happy carefree Noble Savage is a myth. In NEFA at least the people had not enough food; they suffered from abominable diseases; they died young; they were heavily burdened with anxiety; their life was distracted by war, kidnapping, slavery and cruel punishments. They were not even free : weaker tribes had to pay tribute to the strong; rich and powerful Chiefs grew richer on the labour of hundreds of serfs; freedom of movement was severely restricted by inter-village conflict.

And thirdly, while isolation was possible in the last century, it is impossible today. Modern industry is transforming the whole world; the humanitarian ideals of a welfare state no longer permit the neglect of any section of the population; political necessities forbid the existence of any administrative vacuum in the frontier areas; tribal leaders themselves demand greater opportunities. And no one (least of all the scientist) wants to keep the tribal people as museum specimens for the benefit of science.

Yet another criticism is on less solid ground. It has recently been suggested that the Naga rebellion was due to the long isolation in which the people had been kept by the British Government. It has even been suggested that the NEFA Administration is following the same policy, and that this may lead to similarly unhappy results.

It is difficult to agree with this reading of history. The leaders of the Naga National Council, and those who follow them by conviction, are not the Nagas who have had least to do with the outside world, but those who have seen most of it. I myself had long discussions with Shri Phizo in 1947 and one of the chief reasons he then gave for his attitude was the scorn, the exploitation, and the discourtesy which his people suffered from the people of the plains. Many of the rebel Nagas have travelled in other parts of India; Phizo himself has had very wide contacts with the outside world.

So far as NEFA is concerned, the Administration is not, of course, isolating the tribal people at all. Indeed, if it is to be criticised, it might rather be on the ground that it is bringing them a little too quickly into the main stream of modern life. It is pressing forward everywhere with roads which will make the plains easier of access; it is encouraging both the national language and Assamese to help the people to communicate more readily with the outside world; it takes school-boys on tours round India and sends parties regularly to New Delhi on great occasions; it is awarding stipends to its outstanding boys and girls to study in various parts of India; its officers are penetrating into the wildest regions with the message that beyond the hills there is a friendly world with a desire to help and serve.

But the NEFA Administration believes that advance in these long-neglected areas must be on scientific lines. When a man breaks a long fast, he is not immediately given a full meal; he takes a sip of orange-juice. Otherwise he may fall seriously ill. To learn from history, to follow the universally accepted principles of sociological science, to dig firm foundations is not to delay progress; it ensures that *real* progress will be made.

The Policy of Detribalization

In sharp contrast to the first policy is a second one of assimilation or detribalization. This has now become popular and Christian missionaries, social reformers and village uplifters are following it, sometimes on a large and enthusiastic scale. For this too there is something to be said. The Christian missionaries have produced a number of educated tribesmen who are proving of value of the country, and not least of the NEFA administration. Assimilation into Hindu society has often led to a better way of living and to economic advance.

In general, the supporters of this policy take a rather poor view of tribal life : 'animism' should be replaced by the purer ideals of Christianity or Hinduism; the social organization, the 'vices', the 'superstitions' should go; tribal dress is a mark of inferiority and should be replaced by shorts and shirts, blouses and frocks. You cannot make an omelette without breaking eggs, and the continued existence of the tribes as tribes is regarded as of less importance than the march of civilization.

Detribalization is a possible solution of the future of India's tribesmen. It is simple and easy, and it sometimes works. It has, however, serious disadvantages. Its form of progress is by a break with the past, not by an evolution from it. It tends to make the tribesman ashamed of his own culture and religion and so creates that inferiority complex which is a political as well as a social danger. Although it favours a few gifted individuals, who are able to assimilate the new way of life, it generally deprives the mass of the people of their standards and values without putting anything comparable in their place. All over the world it has been noted that the break-up of tribal society leads to a loss of the tribal virtues and a rapid acquisition of the vices of civilization.

The weakening of tribal solidarity and of the folk-legal sanctions deprives the younger generation of their moorings and sets them adrift in an unfamiliar world. All too often, the arts and crafts, the music and dancing, the former self-reliance and independence, the corporate discipline disappear. At the same time, throughout tribal India there is a tendency towards the transformation of tribes into castes, and these 'castes' are usually at the bottom of the social scale. In areas where free commercial penetration has been permitted, there has been much commercial exploitation, inevitable among a people who but yesterday learnt the use of money and who are simple and trusting.

A detailed account of the dangers of this line of approach has been given in an anonymous memorandum on 'The Impact of Modern Civilization on the Tribal Peoples of Madhya Pradesh', with special reference to the situation in Bastar, a wild tract of country largely inhabited by tribal populations, which presents many parallels to NEFA. From this I take the following extracts:

'On contact with their more advanced neighbours, whether through educational institutions of a secular as well as religious character, such as those of the Missions, or through contact with them in work, such as in the mines, it is a generally observed fact that the result is that the virtues of truth and honesty are lost first. It would seem therefore that the break-up of tribal society inevitably leads to a loss of the tribal virtues and a rapid assimilation of the vices of civilization.

'This is due to the weakening of tribal solidarity and of the folk-legal sanctions. The man who has gone away to the mines, or the youth taken from his community and put into a school, considers himself free of, and, indeed, superior to the laws, regulations and customs of his "backward" parents and relations, and needs little inducement to adopt the vices he sees being practised in the urban civilization into which he has been introduced but which, had he remained with his own people, he would have scorned.

'Not only has contact with a higher civilization this effect in the moral realm, but it is equally disastrous in that of craftsmanship. At a time when soil erosion and declining fertility of the soil is bound to become an ever-increasing cause of anxiety, the developing of cottage industries, as a secondary source of livelihood, becomes increasingly important.

'But at this actual juncture, the very existence of the surviving folk-arts and industries is threatened. At Jagdalpur, one may see the tribal people in the bazaar buying metal and other articles, brought in large quantities by merchants, and which were made in Raipur or even further afield.

'How great is this exploitation by commercial interests of the tribal people may be seen when it is realised that they will walk anything up to forty miles to Jagdalpur or Kondagaon[1] to sell in the bazaar a few eggs, mushrooms or other products for a total value of one or two rupees. When they have acquired this money, representing the whole stock of the profit of their husbandry, they will then spend it on some article which formerly they would

[1] Jagdalpur is the chief town of Bastar, and Kondagaon, in the heart of the Muria country, is a sub-divisional headquarters.

have made for themselves.

'Therefore commercial penetration of these regions, which is going forward at an ever-increasing rate, as roads are developed, is threatening to extinguish, on the one hand, folk-crafts and, on the other hand, draining the region of what little money it may have.

'In the immediate neighbourhood of Kondagaon there are villages occupied by tribal people who are now virtually in process of detribalization. One of the results of this process is that, while it is the declared policy of the Government to abolish casteism, casteism is here in the making. Such tribal people have worked out a caste relationship the one with the other, and all with the structure of the surrounding Hindu population, the result of which is that each one forms a caste below the other, and all below the lowest neighbouring Hindu castes.

'To see this in active operation throws light upon how caste, in many cases, may have arisen in the past, as a result of similar clashes of culture and races, but, other than a matter for observation of great academic interest, it is an undesirable development. For it would mean that as all these tribal peoples become absorbed by their neighbours, they would form lowly castes beneath them, thus perpetuating not only a system which the Government desires to abolish, but a form of helotism and exploitation of the tribal peoples which is contrary to universal ethical standards. This fact alone would suggest the desirability of avoiding the absorption of the tribal peoples and the destruction of their own distinctive civilization.

'Owing to the fact that the tribal people are racially mixed, it is quite evident that from the point of view of heredity they will produce from time to time quite able individuals. But since the overall type tends to belong to a racial matrix which has never anywhere developed an advanced civilization, it is reasonable to assume that in general terms they will not be able to take, as a whole, a leading place in a technological age and a civilization which is more and more urbanized.

'Under these circumstances the tribal peoples, whether as individuals drifting into the surrounding populations, or as deculturized tribes, are destined to be exploited by the more advanced populations if the tribal societies are broken up and if, in addition, an adequate measure of protection for them is not afforded by the Government.

'Therefore cultural penetration, leading to deculturizing of the tribes, is a menace of a very serious order to the well-being of these peoples'.

Anthropological literature is full of warnings of this kind and we will make a serious mistake if we lightly ignore the findings (which so far as I know are almost unanimous) of scientists who have approached the problem without bias and with the sole aim of achieving the best and happiest way of life for the people whom their studies have taught them to respect.

The fundamental point is that tribal society, and even the tribal physique, has been adapted through hundreds of years to a special kind of life in a special environment, and that there is grave danger in upsetting too rapidly the harmony between the two.

For example, Dr Buchi, the Swiss biologist, points out that the pygmy Onges of Little Andaman are perfectly adapted to the tropical sun and the dense forests of their environment. They do not represent an 'old and primitive form'; physically they are not at the beginning but at the end of a specialization. Moreover, their type is not the product of a planless evolution; it is one marvellously adjusted to the world they live in.

'In this high specialization, however, lies also a great danger. The adaptation is not only physical, it is a complete biological adaptation to the given circumstances. Contact with civilization changes these circumstances and causes situations for which these people are not prepared, conditions for which they have no powers of resistance. Changes in their way of living, the introduction of diseases and luxuries previously unknown to them may have a catastrophic effect and may lead to their complete extinction in a short time.

'It is consoling to know that attempts are being made to spare the Onges such a fate. Contact with civilization cannot be avoided today. The authorities, however, are trying their best to keep the destructive influences away and to bring these survivors of a special branch of mankind under control without destroying their normal environment.'

The same point is made by the Danish explorer, Jens Bjerre, in his book *The Last Cannibals*. Contrasting the life of the Kukukukus of New Guinea with that of modern civilized man, he says:

'Their lives are completely different from ours; their modes of feeling and reasoning are unfamiliar. Their world of actuality is a savage and dangerous place where they must fight to survive, and where there are no checks upon their primitive and violent desires. Their other world, the invisible one, is alive with magic and mystery. Yet one cannot fail to be conscious of the fundamental human likenesses between these primitives and ourselves. The Kukukukus accept witchcraft and get drunk on murder, blood-lust and cannibalism; the white man goes to church or to the psychoanalyst or drowns his reason in drink.

'In the last few centuries while civilization has swept, like a tide, over the surface of the earth, over Africa, Asia, America and Australia, and has absorbed or obliterated the culture and behaviour of the old races, we often forget that these primitives, through thousands of years, had developed their own pattern of life, materially and mentally, to fit their environment. They found answers to their problems and riddles of living, answers which gave their lives a meaning and significance. We condemn their answers and their patterns. In a sense we are spiritual cannibals; devouring the alien and unfamiliar beliefs of the primitives and devouring, too, their strength and wealth by commercial exploitation.

'We are the cannibals, and we shall be punished for it, perhaps, some day'.

The Prime Minister's Policy

Is there any way out of this dilemma? We are agreed that the people of NEFA cannot be left in their age-long isolation. We are equally agreed that we can leave no political vacuum along our frontier; that we must bring to an end the destructive practices of inter-tribal war and head-hunting and the morally repugnant practices of slavery, kidnapping of children, imposition of cruel punishments and opium-addiction, none of which are fundamental to tribal culture. We wish to see that the people are well-fed, that they are healthy and enjoy a longer span of life, that fewer babies die, that they have better houses, a higher yield for their labour in the fields, improved techniques for their home-industries.

We would like them to be able to move freely about their own hills and have easy access to the greater India of which at present they know little. We want to bring them into contact with the best people and the finest products of modern India.

Above all, we hope to see as the result of our efforts a spirit of love and loyalty for India, without a trace of suspicion that Government has come into the tribal areas to colonize or exploit, a full integration of mind and heart with the great society of which the tribal people form a part and to whose infinite variety they may make a unique contribution.

And at the same time, we want to avoid the dangers of assimilation and detribalization which have degraded tribal communities in other parts of the world.

Is this possible?

It is not easy, but I think it is possible if we follow the middle way between doing too little and doing too much, on which the genius of the Prime Minister, Shri Jawaharlal Nehru, has set our feet. His policy may be summarized as one which approaches the historical development of tribal life and culture with respect and the people themselves in a spirit of affection and identification that eliminates any possibility of superiority. It would not ignore the past, but would build upon it. It would bring the best things of the modern world to the tribes, but in such a way that these will not destroy the traditional way of life, but will activate and develop all that is good in it.

In a number of remarkable speeches, the Prime Minister has spoken of the strong attraction which he has for the tribal people and has described how he has always approached them 'in a spirit of comradeship and not like someone aloof who had come to look at them, examine them, weigh them, measure them and report about them or try and make them conform to another way of life'.

He has given serious warnings of the dangers of the 'assimilation' approach. Pointing out the disastrous effect of the 'so-called European civilization' on tribal peoples in other parts of the world, 'putting to an end their arts and crafts and their simple ways of living', he has declared that 'now to some extent, there is danger of the so-called Indian civilization having this disastrous effect, if we do not check and apply it in the proper way.' 'We may well succeed in uprooting them from their way of life with its standards and discipline, and give them nothing in its place. We may make them feel ashamed of themselves and their own people and thus they may become thoroughly frustrated and unhappy. They have not got the resilience of human beings accustomed to the shocks of the modern world and so they tend to succumb to this shock'. We must, therefore, be very careful to see that 'in our well-meant efforts to improve them, we do not do them grievous injury'. 'It is just possible that in our enthusiasm for doing good, we may over-shoot the mark and do evil instead.' 'It has often happened in other areas of the world that such contact has been disastrous to the primitive culture and gradually the primitive people thus affected die out.'

'I am alarmed,' he has said again, 'when I see — not only in this country, but in other great countries too — how anxious people are to shape others according to their own image or likeness, and to impose on them their particular way of living.' He has declared that he is not sure which, the modern or the tribal, is the better way of living. 'In some respects I am quite certain their's is better'. 'They possess a variety of cultures and are in many ways certainly not backward.'

'We must cease to think of ourselves as different from the so-called tribal people. This is a vicious idea. It is due to a superiority complex which has no basis in reality. I can say with complete honesty that some of the tribal people have reached a high degree of development. In fact I have found that in some places they are highly educated and disciplined and lead a corporate communal life which, I think, is far better than the caste-ridden society from which we suffer'.

The Prime Minister has further emphasized the importance of encouraging the tribal languages, so that they will not only prevail but flourish. He has insisted that a measure of protection must be given so that 'no outsider can take possession of tribal lands or forests or interfere with them in any way except with their consent and goodwill.' It is his desire that the high sense of discipline, the power to enjoy life, the love of dance and song will endure among them. 'I am anxious that they should advance, but I am even more anxious that they should not lose their artistry and joy in life and the culture that distinguishes them in many ways.'

Schemes for welfare, education, communications, medical relief are no doubt essential; 'one must always remember, however, that we do not mean to interfere with their way of life, but want to help them to live it.' 'The Government of India'—and in this sentence the Prime Minister's entire policy is epitomized—'is determined to help the tribal people to grow according to their own genius and tradition; it is not the intention to impose anything on them.'

Shri Jairamdas Daulatram, former Governor of Assam, has expressed the same idea in other words.

'Each section of our large population,' he once said, 'contributes to the making of the nation in the same manner as each flower helps to make a garden. Every flower has the right to grow according to its own laws of growth; has the right to enrich and develop its own colour and form and to spread its own fragrance to make up the cumulative beauty and splendour of the garden. I would not like to change my roses into lilies nor my lilies into roses. Nor do I want to sacrifice my lovely orchids and rhododendrons of the hills'.

And the present Governor of Assam, Shri Fazl Ali, describing the tribal people of Orissa, spoke in 1952 of their simplicity, their community life and their integrity.

'Many eminent people who understand human values have been fascinated by these qualities, and it is up to us to see that they are not crushed and destroyed by the load of poverty, disease and starvation or by outside corrupting influences. The aim of our Welfare State should be to let these natural and unsophisticated people continue to sing and dance and laugh as nature expects them to do, and yet to so order their life that they may become, in course of time, useful members of society and a source of strength to the State.'

In a similar spirit Pandit G. B. Pant, Union Home Minister of India, has emphasized the contribution that the tribal people can make to the life of the country. He is reported as saying in a recent conference at Koraput that:

'India is a vast country with a rich variety of culture and topography and in this scene of diversity our tribal brethren occupy a very important place. The tribal people have been truly described as an artistic creation of God passionately devoted to their own way of life. They express their joy of life through the colourful forms of their folk-dances and the rhythm of their music.

'Their frankness, love of truth and unshakable loyalty to those who win their confidence are well known. They are literally sons of the soil, and the skill with which they create neat and clean habitations and meet the other requirements of life are a matter for admiration.

'It is wrong, therefore, to consider these people less civilized or backward. They are our own kinsmen and non-tribals can learn many good lessons from their way of life.'

This original, indeed unique, conception, at once scientific and humane, steers a middle path between the two older ways of approach and, if properly applied, should have the advantages of both and avoid their dangers.

It is not an easy policy. The assimilation or detribalization policy, which held, as we have seen, that there is not very much to be said for tribal life; that if it disappears, it will not matter greatly; that the 'backward' must be brought forward and the 'low' uplifted, is simple and straightforward; it is logical and it brings certain benefits — at a price. So did the old British policy of leaving well alone, though at a different price.

But there can be no doubt that the Prime Minister's policy is the right one. It is supported both by the findings of anthropological science and the warnings of history. It is a charter of religious, social, economic and cultural rights. It is the embodiment of the spirit of reverence. It is the gospel of friendliness and equality. It is the gate whereby the tribal people may enter into full union with the India of which they form so important and valuable a part.

Today we can see tribal peoples without sentiment, but equally without prejudice. Isolation in the modern world is impossible; it would not be desirable even if it was possible. The old controversy about zoos and museums has long been dead. We do not want to preserve tribal culture in its colour and beauty to interest the scientists or attract the tourists. To try to preserve and develop the best elements in tribal art, religion and culture is something very different from wishing to keep the people in a zoo.

We do not want to preserve the tribesmen as museum specimens, but equally we do not want to turn them into clowns in a circus. We do not want to stop the clock of progress, but we do want to see that it keeps the right time. We do not accept the myth of the Noble Savage; but we do not want to create a class of Ignoble Serfs.

We see now that the tribal people will be of the greatest service to India if they are able to bring their own peculiar treasures into the common life, not by becoming second-rate copies of ourselves. Their moral virtues, their self-reliance, their courage, their artistic gifts, their cheerfulness are things we need. They also need the comradeship, the technical knowledge, the wider world-view of the plains. The great problem is how to develop the synthesis, how to bring the blessings and advantages of modern medicine, agriculture and education to them, without destroying the rare and precious values of tribal life.

We can solve this problem if we do not try to go too fast: if we allow the people a breathing-space in which to adjust themselves to the new world: if we do not overwhelm them with too many officials; if we aim at fundamentals and eliminate everything that is not vitally necessary; if we go to them in genuine love and true simplicity. In a word, if we follow the Prime Minister's policy, there is a chance we may succeed; if we do not, it is certain we will fail.

Part Two

MATERIAL AIMS IN NEFA

India, like other underdeveloped countries of the world, is a poor country. The majority of the people are underfed, under-employed or unemployed. They lack proper housing, clothing, sanitation and the like. Living under these uncongenial conditions, they have almost lost the faculty of clear thinking. It will indeed be a wastage of effort if we try to teach people about proper dietary requirements when they do not have the means to procure even one good meal a day. There seems to be no use in trying to teach them what an ideal home should be like or what should be the proper sanitary measures when they are hungry and without adequate clothing or shelter. The basic requirements must be supplied first before we think of educating them. Adequate employment must be provided for every individual so that he can earn his living in the most modest way by honest labour and not through charity. Charity can alleviate distress or poverty for the time being, but cannot be a permanent solution of the problem. On the other hand charity makes a man lose his moral strength and confidence in his own ability.

—ASHADEVI ARYANAYAKAM

Mahatma Gandhi, talking (so far as I remember) to a young man who was a little too exclusively interested in culture, once declared that 'the masses need only one poem — invigorating food.' The material aims of NEFA must necessarily therefore take the first place, for the people are often hungry and often sick. There is nothing more important than the provision of concrete material benefits for the common man.

Yet even here the first of our material aims is at least partially a psychological one. We want the people to produce more food: if they are to do this with enthusiasm, they must feel that they own the land they cultivate. In other parts of India, where the tribal communities have declined in many ways, the first cause of their depression was the loss of their land and forests. This had the effect of so enervating the tribal organism that it had no interior resistance against infection by a score of other evils. A Bishop was once talking to Samuel Johnson about the poor. 'They grow quite torpid,' he said, 'for want of property.' And Johnson replied, 'They have no object for hope. Their condition cannot be bettered. It is rowing without a port.'

The Problem of Land

To the tribal mind, our attitude about land and forests is as important as any scheme of development or education. If we look back over the long series of rebellions against authority in other parts of tribal India, we see that the majority of them arose over this one point. Thus the Kol insurection of 1833 was caused by encroachment on tribal land. The Tamar rebellions, repeated seven times between 1789 and 1832, were primarily due to the illegal deprivation of their rights in land which Hos, Mundas and Uraons had suffered.

The story of the great Santal rebellion has been told by Dr J. H. Hutton in *Modern India and the West.* He shows how the excellent original intentions of Government to protect the people were eroded by the tide of civilization, so that gradually all the best land passed into the hands of outsiders. And elsewhere a missionary, the Rev. W. J. Culshaw, has written well on the same theme:

'The most powerful motive in Santal life is possession of the land which they till. Land belongs to those by whom the original clearings in the forest were made, and passes through the male line to their descendants — remaining always within the same clan. The Santal village officials received special lands as recognition of their services and of their office. No motive is so strong in a tribal people as the preservation of the life of the tribe and its mores, albeit the motive works for the most part at the unconscious level; and a Santal's land not only provides economic security, but is a powerful link with his ancestors; and this applies to newly-entered areas no less than the old, for he will not take possession till the spirits approve. The land is a part of his spiritual as well as his economic heritage.

'Hunger drove the Santals to despair, but their attachment to the land provided also an emotional basis without which the rebellion might not have taken place.'

The Rampa rebellion in East Godavari was for the same cause, so at bottom was the Bastar rising of 1911. A comparatively recent rebellion in the Adilabad District of Hyderabad in 1941 was due partly to the alienation of Gond land, partly to the reservation of forests which was extended over all areas which were not actually under cultivation at the time. Thereby a great deal of land which had in former years been cultivated in rotation and which at the time of demarcation was lying fallow, was included in the Reserves and the tribal people were deprived of its future use. Many Gonds and Kolams were expelled from their ancestral lands and were forced to seek a living by working for non-tribals. They rebelled in despair.

In NEFA much of the land is held traditionally on a corporate basis; it belongs to the village rather than to individuals, and in the past there have been many feuds over the drawing of boundary-lines between different village areas. Jhum-cultivation naturally creates a situation different from that in settled areas, where a family cultivates the same plot of land year after year. In some cases, it is true, the people claim rather more than their share — great tracts of hill and forest which in their small numbers they can never hope to cultivate. But it is of the first importance that we should guarantee to them all the land and forest which they traditionally use, allowing generously for future expansion and increase of population.

It is interesting that the first attempt by the former British Government to give some protection to the tribal people in Assam was connected with this problem. In 1873 the Inner Line Regulation was enacted, not with the aim (as is so often thought) of isolating the hill people from the plains, but to bring 'under more stringent control the commercial relations of British subjects with the frontier tribes'. In Lakhimpur the operations of speculators in caoutchouc had led to serious complications, and the spread of Tea Gardens beyond the fiscal limits of the settled territories of the day had involved Government in many conflicts with the hillmen. The Inner Line Regulation, therefore, enacted that no British subject or foreign resident could pass beyond a certain point without a licence; it also laid down rules concerning trade and the possession of land beyond the Line. And indeed for a long time to come it will be necessary to give some measure of protection to the people of NEFA if they are not to suffer the fate of their brethren elsewhere.

The Problem of the Forests

This leads us on to the problem of the forests. I have myself recorded the melancholy story of the effect of reservation on the Baigas of Madhya Pradesh in my book on that tribe. Nothing roused the Saoras of Orissa to such resentment against Government as the taking from them of forests which they regarded as their own property. Of the Bhuiyas and Juangs of Bonai and Keonjhar, I wrote in a report in 1942:

'It is necessary for us to appreciate the attitude of the aboriginal. To him the hills and forests are his. Again and again it was said to me, "These hills are ours; what right has anyone to interfere in our own property?"

'Before this claim is dismissed as wholly fantastic, we would do well to remember that had these folk the wit and education to make regular claims at the time of the early settlements, they might today be legally settled in the possession of the great estates on which they have lived for centuries. I do not suppose the courts would uphold their claims today—but if they have no legal rights, they surely have considerable moral rights in the areas they have possessed so long. They have lived in these remote and inaccessible hills, racked by malaria, fighting a constant battle against wild beasts and unfriendly Nature, paying their State dues year after year and receiving literally nothing by way of public services in return, and yet no rights or liberties are legally granted to them.'

Some words by Dr Hutton may also be considered:

'The restriction of jhuming in the Kond Maliahs of Orissa has more than once resulted in civil disturbance, if not in the active rebellion of the whole Kond tribe, while the Chenchus farther south have suffered much as the Baigas have. In Assam, Government has adopted the same attitude towards shifting cultivation that it did in the Central Provinces and denied any title to land not under permanent cultivation. This attitude, however, has rarely been enforced in practice in the hill districts. If the Assam Forest Regulations, under which tribal land used for jhum cultivation is treated as Unclassed State Forest, were to be strictly enforced all

2

over Assam, they would undoubtedly cause such widespread discontent and privation as to lead to open rebellion.'

Of the tribal groups of Bombay State a Census Officer of 1931 wrote as follows:

The reactions of the Forest Laws on the Hill and Aboriginal Tribes have been considerable. Previous to the creation of the Forest Department, Hill Tribes roamed the forest areas more or less at will and were generally the sole purveyors of forest produce. . . . It is true that the Forest Department employs a fair number of the forest folk but the actual net benefit derived by them from the existence of a systematized administration is probably a good deal less than the profits formerly obtained from the almost uncontrolled exploitation of forest areas and is thus poor consolation to a simple and illiterate member of the Hill and Aboriginal Tribes, whose solitary desire is to live and let live.'

This will be sufficient to emphasize the extreme value, both material and religious, attached to the land and the forest by the tribesmen elsewhere: the feeling in NEFA is, if anytning, even stronger. A recognition of this must be the background of any attempt on our part to solve the problem.

We may well remember the words of Sir Bampfylde Fuller (in 1901): 'It is of much more importance that a tribe of people should live in peace and comfort, than that a certain area of land should grow trees of one sort or indeed should grow trees at all.'

The present forest policy in NEFA is one of exceptional liberality and is based on the Administration's circular which declares that it 'must be conditioned by the direct interests of the people and not by our desire to increase revenue by launching upon a policy of exploitation of forests identical with that in other parts of the country.' The Senior Officers Conference in 1955 recommended that the existing regulations should be made even more elastic, that the tribal people should be given freedom to extract timber and other products from reserved forests for their own use, that they should be allowed to hunt and fish freely except during the breeding season, and even that those of them who are settled within a reserved forest area should be allowed to acquire more land within the reserve if this was necessary for their subsistence.

Freedom to hunt and fish is of the first importance; the loss of this freedom has been a major cause of tribal decline in other parts of India. In the old days in the Central Provinces, Forest Officers collected and burnt the bows and arrows of the Gonds and Baigas. At the same time, officials and other outsiders were freely allowed to shoot the animals which the people considered to be their's.

In NEFA, there are two considerations which we must keep in mind. The first is that, except in certain unpopulated areas, the wild life is in danger of being completely exterminated. There are great tracts of country where it is difficult to hear even the song of a bird. Unless, therefore, we do something quickly to protect this wild life, it will disappear altogether within a few years, and this will not only be bad in itself, but it will be a serious loss to the people who have always depended on hunting and fishing to supplement their diet with badly-needed food values.

Secondly we must remember that the entire tribal area is divided into what we may call zones of influence; every tribe, every village has forests and streams over which it claims hunting and fishing rights, and there have been serious disputes and even wars as a result of their infringement. Then, all over tribal India, hunting and fishing is something more than a search for food: it is a religious activity involving strict taboos; on the success or failure of a ceremonial hunt will depend the success or failure of the harvest; the horns of an animal, the bones of a big fish, are hung up in the hunter's house, and it is taboo to desecrate them; before and after a hunt, offerings are made to the forest gods.

Under these circumstances, it is not surprising that the people should resent the incursion of outsiders to take the animals and fish which they regard as their own and which are bound to them by mythological and religious ties. In the old days, when there were only a few officers, the fact that a Political Officer went round with his gun raised no difficulties and in fact the people appreciated the excitement of an 'official hunt'; the older officers too were careful to divide any game with the local villagers.

But with a great increase in staff, it may well happen that too many officers will want to hunt and fish and what is a necessity for the tribal folk will be sacrificed for what is after all a luxury for us. For this reason we have asked our Political Officers to be very careful in issuing shooting licences and have appealed to all members of our staff to reduce their shooting and fishing to a minimum.

Tribal people everywhere are meticulously careful about the division of meat, and at feasts and festivals, after a successful hunt, the meat and other food is always divided according to certain traditional rules. When, on the rare occasions that an officer does go hunting and is successful, it would, therefore, be a courteous and appropriate gesture for him to distribute a good proportion of the game (in my opinion it should be at least half) to the tribesmen in whose forests he has hunted.

We hope gradually to educate the people to observe close seasons for certain types of animal, to kill animals for sacrifice in a more merciful manner and to give up the practice of fishing by poison. But in this we have to be extremely careful, for any suspicion that we are trying to interfere with hunting and fishing rights will have immediate and unfavourable political consequences.

To make up for any deficiency in the meat diet as a result of less hunting, we are doing all we can to improve the quality of the live-stock; veterinary centres have been opened, and new breeds of cattle, pigs and fowls have been introduced.

All this sufficiently indicates the concern of the Administration for tribal interests. But it must be remembered that a policy of this kind is temporary; it might be reversed in future years, and a less generous policy in the future might have all the more serious repercussions just because of today's liberality.

The people of NEFA cannot be spoon-fed and coddled for ever. If they are to be strong, they must emerge one day from their seclusion and battle on equal terms with the outside world. Before this happens it is essential that we should provide them with clear titles to their lands and forests, so that even though the protecting hand of the present Administration may be withdrawn, they will be comparatively secure.

Some of the tribes who later suffered the most abominable exploitation from outsiders were at the beginning in a position not unlike that of our NEFA tribes today. They were protected by their seclusion, by their own intractibility, by a measure of administrative beneficence. But time passed; communications were improved, the people themselves grew tame, the fostering care of

Government was withdrawn. And because they had been insufficiently established in their ownership, they gradually lost much of their land and so fell into poverty and despair.

Some of the older British officials pleaded for the granting of greater proprietory or ownership rights over land to the tribesmen. Their voices were largely unheeded — with tragic results. I believe that history will judge us primarily on two things: how we solve the problem of tribal culture, and how we deal with the problem of tribal land.

Communications and Food

Among our material aims, we have given top priority to communications and food. We cannot for ever depend on the airlift which has made the opening up of NEFA possible. For the tribal people roads, paths, bridges mean that in the new era of peace they will be able to get about; fresh possibilities of trade will open to them; in times of scarcity they will get supplies more quickly; through the roads they will become more closely linked with the rest of India and will get to know it better. And in particular good bridges over the rivers will mean a great expansion of inter-village amity in the interior; hitherto villages on opposite banks of an unfordable river have had little to do with one another — and when we don't know someone we tend to scorn or dislike him.

Communications will probably even assist in solving our language problem, for as the people are able to move about more freely they may evolve a sort of NEFA Esperanto, and the multiplicity of dialects, which grew up largely as a result of the difficulty of communications, will disappear and only the great essential languages will survive.

There is obviously nothing more important than to make NEFA self-sufficient in food, for the people are often short of essential food-stuffs although, like tribal folk everywhere, they are remarkably adept in supplementing their diet with the forest produce which Mother Nature in her mercy provides.

The people of NEFA nearly all practice shifting cultivation (jhuming) and this is closely linked with their mythology, their social customs and even their religion. The Administration has wisely refused to forbid the practice, which in some States has been stopped altogether to the distress and indignation of the tribesmen. It is probable that the evil effects of jhuming — erosion and destruction of the forest — have been exaggerated, for if sufficient rotation is allowed, and in a thinly populated area like NEFA there is no reason why there should not be a long period for rotation, the forest recovers well enough. And in many parts it is unlikely that it will ever be possible to find a substitute, the hills are so steep and the water scarce.

But we are trying to introduce terracing and wet-rice-cultivation wherever possible and have met with some success. We have to remember, however, that this depends on a suitable terrain as well as on tactful, and persuasive education.

The most important thing is that our officers should not, in their enthusiasm for new methods, give the impression that the Administration disapproves of jhuming. We ought not to speak of it as an 'evil'. This might well have political repercussions and give rise to the suspicion that we wish to take away the village land. Moreover vegetables and pulses are grown in the jhums and for a long time to come this ought to be encouraged. The ideal is to allow both permanent and shifting cultivation to continue side by side. This is what happens in the Saora Hills of Orissa, and the Saoras are, as a result, one of the most prosperous and best fed of all the central Indian tribes. Rice is grown on the terraces and irrigated fields, and other crops in the jhums; some such solution may be found in NEFA.

Our attitude to shifting cultivation well illustrates the 'Middle Way' we are trying to follow. One way of dealing with the problem is to forbid jhuming altogether — this is an undue interference in the life of the people and causes psychological and material impoverishment. Another way, followed in the past, was to permit it without check. This too was wrong, for there are various ways in which jhuming can be improved and the damage to the forest alleviated.

The NEFA Administration is attempting a far-reaching agricultural reform — but from within. It does not forbid jhuming, but it is teaching improved methods within the traditional framework. It hopes to lessen the danger of erosion by increasing the cycle of rotation and by teaching the people to plant seedlings in clearings. At the same time. it is introducing new methods of terracing and irrigation: it is encouraging vegetable gardens and growing of fruit trees; it is distributing new labour-saving implements and better seed. Here is an interesting instance of how modern science can assist tribal economy without destroying it.

Self-sufficiency in Cloth

To achieve self-sufficiency in cloth is another matter of high priority. We may remember that throughout his life Mahatma Gandhi placed khadi in the forefront of his programme: to Jawaharlal Nehru it was 'the livery of our freedom.' In NEFA, however, the spinning-wheel is little known; not much cotton is grown and for the time being we are being cautious in diverting attention to it from food crops until the goal of self-sufficiency in food is attained. On the other hand, some tribes spin a strong and durable yarn from bark fibre; others spin wool obtained from Tibet; the bark cloth and woollen cloth in the northern hills is aesthetically pleasing, durable and warm. The Administration is taking steps to encourage this industry in every way possible.

Many tribes have a tradition of weaving and some of them weave very well indeed. In other areas weaving has either never existed or has perished before the competition of mill-made goods. We are now making an all-out effort to revive it where it does not exist and to encourage and develop it where it does. If we can do this, we shall help to solve the problem of tribal dress; we shall make the people largely independent of the merchants from the plains; we will keep a lot of money inside NEFA; and we will stimulate an essential medium of artistic expression.

To achieve this the import of cotton and woollen yarn has been arranged on a large scale to sell in our shops and emporiums, and there has been a good deal of research to ensure that yarn of the right count and correct colour is provided. We are sending mobile training units into villages where weaving is not known, and we are starting a number of co-operative production centres.

Here is another 'material' aim which will have important psychological and even political results. The book *Hand-Spinning and Hand-Weaving* was written a long time ago, but the following passage is as relevant today as when it was first composed.

'The village craftsman and artisan is far more healthy and enjoys better surroundings than his brother, the mill worker. The smaller wage earned by him is more than compensated by the habit of contentment developed in cottage surroundings. The future of the country rests truly with the village artisan. He has to recharge the whole psychological atmosphere of his home with creative energy.

'The handloom weaver will have to display his marvellous skill in work and design and find free vent for his individuality. There is great hope that this will come to be. The craftsman of the future years will naturally be fastidious in respect of material which he owns and on which he expends his labour and skill and the more so since he will be personally responsible for the quality of the finished product. Becoming a free agent in production he will enrich the national taste and safeguard it against decay. His hands being full of work, he will use his talent to best advantage. Not being cramped in body and soul he will make the citizen of the future and help in the rebuilding of the manhood of the nation.

'An industry with a new economic and cultural outlook will have been revived and then and not till then will the nation become the nursery of the beautiful, and cease to suffer from the twin diseases of "standardized minds and standardized commodities".'

The same attitude has recently been emphasized by the Prime Minister in a conversation with an English journalist, John Strachey, which was reported in *The New Statesman*.

STRACHEY: 'To the student of your Second Five-Year Plan the most striking thing about it is that the plan proposes development of two opposite kinds, as it were. On the one hand you are beginning to build up the very latest types of large-scale modern industry — for instance I have just seen your new locomotive-building workshop at Chittaranjan, your fertilizer plant at Sindri and your 120-feet seam of open-cast coal at Bokaro. But then, on the other hand, and at the same time, you propose not only to preserve but actually to develop your cottage industry — you propose to extend the spinning and weaving of textiles by hand, on hand-spindles and handlooms. I realise that all this may be quite right and logical in Indian conditions, but it is certainly startling.

NEHRU: 'Yes, I know. But you must remember two things. First, hand-spinning and weaving — specially handloom weaving

— is by no means dead in India. There are still many thousands of handlooms being worked in cottages throughout the country. We believe that this deep Indian tradition of handicrafts must not be allowed to die out. We believe that it can be developed most fruitfully. Then, again, the spinning and weaving of textiles by hand is an integral part of the whole nationalist tradition of which the Congress Party has been the leader and organizer. For instance, I am quite a good spinner. I used to like to use the hand-spindle. I found it an interesting and skilled occupation — splendid relaxation from mental activity.'

NEHRU: 'On the other hand handloom weaving, rather than spinning, is the more promising process for our cottage industry development.'

STRACHEY: 'What about the economics of the thing? Can the handloom possibly compete?'

NEHRU: 'Do not draw hasty conclusions about this. Remember that there may be great economies for the country as a whole in this cottage industry, and in particular in handloom weaving. There are economies in transport. Not only is the raw material often produced next door, in the same village where it is spun and woven, but also there are great social advantages in not herding millions of men and women into the great cities in order to mobilize them for large-scale machine industry. Think of the vast resources which India would have to put into city transport and other public services, if she were to develop all of her industries in the cities. Only a country which is planning its development on a socialist pattern can take into account these major social economics. For they do not affect the individual firm, since the individual firm does not have to pay for these developments of public utilities, city housing, and transport. But the country does have to pay for them — so there may be great advantages in cottage industries after all.'

The Development of Cottage Industries

Allied with this is the development of cottage industries in general. We have established in all the divisions Cottage Industries Training and Production Centres (CITPC's), whose aim is not to create new 'castes' of carpenters, blacksmiths, potters and so on, but to enrich village life by giving the trainees a subsidiary occupation which they will take home and teach to their fellows.

An important aspect of these institutions has been a new stress on production as well as, and in some respects instead of, training. For example, there is no particular point in importing into NEFA some inexperienced young man to teach cane and bamboo work at which the tribal people are already expert. There is no need to spend Government money to teach students to do badly what they already do well. Weaving-schools in areas where there is already a high tradition of weaving have sometimes done more harm than good. The effect on the girls has often been unfortunate; designs have been debased; and in practice little has been achieved. It is another matter where the weaving tradition has perished, and in such areas our weaving-schools have done very useful work.

The fly-shuttle loom, for all its advantages, is not suitable for NEFA. It is too large for the houses and it is a fixture. Tribal women like to take their looms out into the sun whenever they can. Instead we are introducing the simpler Assamese loom, which greatly increases output, on which many of the tribal designs can be made, and which has the advantage of being portable; some training in this will be necessary, after which we can swich over mainly to production.

In order to introduce new crafts, such as conventional carpentery, ironmongery, pottery, it is necessary to bring instructors from outside, but so far as possible we plan to entrust the teaching of wood-carving, or cane and bamboo work to local men.

For example, where wood-carving is being introduced, we are arranging to engage first-class wood-carvers from among the Monpas, Wanchos, Khamptis, Konyaks, or whatever tribe may be able to produce them, and let them teach the boys to carve in the traditional style. Otherwise if a wood-carver is engaged from the plains, he is likely to do as much harm as good, for at that level I doubt if it will be possible to find anyone who would be humble enough to let the boys 'develop along the lines of their own genius'. In the Santal Parganas, I have noticed the disastrous effect of standardized urban wood-carving on the Santals, whose traditional carving is remarkable for its strength and originality. The new style is beautifully tidy with geometrical patterns and inspiringly symmetrical — but it is dead.

The introduction of wood-carving, as separate from carpentery, in the CITPC's is most important. There is a danger that this art, at which some of the people excel, may die out — partly because in Tirap and Tuensang at least it was so closely associated with head-hunting. In Kameng trainees are being taught to make their own masks for pantomimes on the model of those carved at Tawang, and this will not only save themselves money and encourage a remarkable type of dancing but, once local needs have been supplied, will certainly find a ready market elsewhere. The same will be true of the toys, decorated beer-mugs, carved pipes and combs and other objects made in Tirap and Tuensang, the making of which we hope to revive.

But these things will have little or no sale unless they are genuine products of tribal creativeness.

In the same way, Hatters Sections in the CITPC's will help to preserve one of the objects of tribal dress about which there can be little controversy. The hats can be improved — especially in regard to their weight. For hitherto a hat has been in the nature of a crash-helmet, heavy and cumbersome to ward off the blows of enemies, and now that peace has come, the hats may well be made of lighter material, even though there is no need to alter the essential design.

Unhappily, in the cane-work sections of the CITPC's there is what is perhaps a natural tendency to lay too much emphasis on making such things as IN and OUT trays for offices.

In the field of cottage industries, a great deal depends on the initiative and imagination of the senior officers. The enthusiasm of the Political Officer at Bomdila has resulted in a first-class institution, which is a model of its kind. The Weaving Class is producing quantities of excellent cloth with the beautiful traditional designs; wood-carvers are making the local bowls and cups, and artists are painting them. Round the official buildings are small houses where local craftsmen are plying their trade. Everything is homely, natural, and thus effective.

In Siang too there has been a renaissance of weaving (and of dancing) among the Gallongs, largely inspired by the CITPC at Along. Good progress has been made in weaving in the Nocte area of Tirap where the art had died out, and simple looms and good cane chairs are made at Namsang of a type that will be useful to the people themselves.

Allied with the Training and Production Centres are Village

Co-operative and Weaving Societies, which have made a good start. We are building up these on the foundation of the strongly self-reliant and co-operative character of the people. A tribal village is itself a co-operative society in embryo; in many ways it lives and works as a single unit. In these Societies there is to be a maximum of simplicity and a minimum of complicated financial rules.

Medical Aid

Medical work in NEFA has had to face serious difficulty in the shortage of doctors and the indifference of the people to scientific treatment. Here the personal equation is of paramount importance. Some of the people make long journeys to the plains to take their troubles to Mission Hospitals, not out of any attachment to Mission religion, but because, so they say, they are treated with love, consideration and efficiency. Every patient who prefers a Mission Hospital to one of ours is a challenge and a reproach.

In my experience — and I have visited many dispensaries in the far interior — wherever a doctor takes the right approach and gives himself to the people, his work is a success. But a doctor who goes merely for a job (and of course this applies to every member of the staff), does not bother to learn a language, spends his time grumbling about his pay and lack of facilities and amenities, who does not, in short, love the people and give himself to them in a spirit of sacrifice and devotion, is a failure.

There are many other aspects of our programme for material benefit and I cannot discuss them all. The improvement of the water-supply is one of the most urgent needs for a people who in many cases prefer to locate their villages on the tops of hills, far away from a stream. Lack of water means dirt, disease and waste of time. If the time spent in climbing laboriously up and down hills to a water-point could be used for weaving or some other gainful employment, it would be a great advantage.

Some of the tribes (such as the Monpas and Khamptis) make ingenious water-mills for grinding or husking grain, and we plan to introduce these in areas where they are not known. They will be of great value in saving the women's time and labour, and we hope to make them in the local style so that they will fit into the general village picture.

Carpentery illustrates one of the many problems that we have to face. The original idea was that we should teach our carpenter trainees to make only, or mainly, those things, such as ploughs and doors, which would be useful in their own homes. But official demands for furniture, not only for the staff but for scores of institutions, have become so heavy that we have had to choose between importing a large number of carpenters from outside and utilizing the tribal boys to fulfil the demand. A modification of policy has thus been inevitable, and for some years to come tribal boys will have plenty of work as carpenters with a constant official market for their products, though we are continuing to stress the importance of relating their work to village needs.

Essential Principles

In all our material aims we have to bear certain points in mind. The first is that we should base everything, as far as possible, on the local economy. It is no use introducing cane-work in a school if the cane has to be flown in by the Indian Air Force (at one time this was actually done). It is useless to provide seedlings which will not thrive in the wrong altitude. It is no good bringing in delicate animals which cannot stand the climate. Yarn is the one exception to this: we will have to import it for some time to come.

Secondly, we must work, and we are planning to work, through the local institutions. For co-operatives we propose to use the local village council such as the Kebang in Siang and western Lohit. I suggest in a later section ways in which our doctors may utilize the services of the tribal priests. Our agricultural programmes will succeed better if members of the staff share in the local agricultural ceremonies and festivals.

And then we must be, indeed we are now being, careful not to pauperize, a subject to which I return later. Subsidies for agriculture are to my mind a risky enterprise, for if once the tribesmen get the idea that Government is going to pay for everything they will soon cease to do anything for themselves. The people of NEFA are not nearly as poor as is commonly supposed, and some of them now are making quite a lot of money. To get things free has never yet been good for anyone.

And finally, in all this effort we have to balance the material gains against psychological factors. We must bear in mind the Prime

Minister's warnings that we are not to over-do it, that we may in our eagerness to do good do grievous harm instead, that we may overwhelm the people by sheer weight of numbers. There will be little advantage in being able to say that we have appointed so many Village Level Workers (horrid expression) if these, by slackness or by interference in tribal customs stir up resentment against the Administration. It will be no use introducing a new craft if the instructors offend tribal sentiment and ultimately cause political agitation.

Nor is there any point in merely putting more and more money into the hands of the people if they do not spend that money wisely, and if its possession means that they give up work in their fields. Already there is a disquieting movement to buy grain instead of growing it. Instead of spending money on live-stock, cows which will give the children milk, better seeds and other ways of enriching life, there is a tendency to spend it on unnecessary and even harmful things. Nor will the introduction of cinemas and radio-sets, football and scouting, recreation centres and volunteer camps be of ultimate benefit if at the same time the people lose their traditional virtues of truth and honesty, discipline and self-reliance, and their own traditional forms of recreation.

In every expansion programme there are two points of view. One is to increase staff and institutions regardless of quality on the principle that 'Something is better than Nothing'. The other is to go slowly and carefully, laying sound foundations, on the principle that 'It is better to do a little well than to do a lot badly'. I have no doubt whatever that in the tribal areas the second view is to be preferred. The total absence of a bee-keeper, a sericulturalist or a pigling multiplication farm will not cause any trouble. But if we send an inefficient bee-keeper, a lazy sericulturalist, if our piglings decrease rather than multiply, or if we start something that we cannot implement, a very bad impression may be caused. As the Adviser, Shri K. L. Mehta, has said: 'There is little point in laying down targets which are unachievable and making promises which cannot be fulfilled'.

Above all, we must not be dominated by statistics: we must realise that it is not the number of boys in a school or of trainees in a hostel that matters, but the quality of life and character which is created.

One of our most difficult problems is how to balance the need to solve urgent, even dramatic, human problems against the equally important need of not overwhelming the local people with too large an importation of official staff. However warmly they may welcome the occasional visitor, tribal people everywhere are fundamentally zenophobic; they do not like having outsiders, even nice outsiders, about too much. The Prime Minister has noted this recently:

'What I am anxious about particularly is to avoid large numbers of outsiders being sent to the tribal areas in some capacity or other. If that happens, however well we may train them, the mere numbers will produce what I would call a revolutionary situation in the tribal areas. We will lose grip of the situation then and will have to content ourselves with drifting and accepting many things that we do not like.

'I have said above that even if we train all the people we send there, the consequences are likely to be bad. It is obvious, however, that we cannot give adequate training to every minor official who is sent there. Some of our people who go there look upon the tribals in a superior way. They make fun of them and sometimes they run after their women-folk. All this creates a multitude of problems'.

One of the ways in which we are trying to solve this problem is by making many of our officers 'multipurpose' in function, so that a Base Superintendent, for example, can do the work of an Inspector of Schools in addition to his own duties when he is on tour. Another way is to weed out the inefficient and the unsuitable. Yet another is to use the local people as far as possible. Challenging human problems, such as, for example, the abolition of slavery, the checking of opium-addiction, the cure of the terrible dermatitis that affects some of the northern tribes, demand men, and men of the highest quality, but we constantly keep in mind the danger of a mere multiplication of officials. We remember that Gandhiji used to say that the best Government was the Government that governed least.

Part Three

THE PROBLEM OF DRESS

I am horrified at the picture of these people being made to give up their old artistic clothes or even lack of clothes in favour of a dirty pair of shorts or some such thing. I am also greatly disturbed at certain shabby articles of modern civilization replacing the artistic products of these people. I am quite clear that we should prevent cheap mill-cloth going there as far as we can. We are in fact encouraging hand-spun and hand-woven goods all over India. Surely we should use only these in this area for presents and for other purposes. Indeed the right course would be to get yarn woven into artistic patterns and encourage this artistic craft there.

I do not agree with the criticism that the preservation of tribal art and tribal dress indicates a desire to keep the tribal people as museum specimens. The danger is that these people will lose their culture and have nothing to replace it. I have no doubt that with the opening out of roads and other communications, these remote areas will be influenced by the rest of India. What has usually happened is that these artistic primitive people lose their artistry and get nothing to replace it. I would rather that they remain museum specimens than become such representatives of so-called modern progress. Of course I do not wish them to feel that we are stopping the 'clock of progress', though I have my grave doubts as to whether this clock is one of progress or not. We do not wish to stop them from doing what they like, but we must not encourage them to go the wrong way.

—JAWAHARLAL NEHRU

I have given an important place to the subject of Dress, for it is a symbol of so many things and raises in a concentrated form most of the problems that we have to face in other matters.

It is a commonplace that dress is something much more than a mere protection of the body against the weather. It is a form of art, on which some of the finest minds of all nations have lavished their attention. It is a symbol, whereby a man's social status can be determined. Like the feathers of birds, to which it is so often compared, it is a form of allure leading to mating between the sexes. Although today we live in a drab and ugly world, where the dress of men at least has lost its former bravery, there were times in the past, and there may again be times in the future, when clothes will regain their colour and beauty.

'Fashion', says James Laver, 'sums up all the subterranean tendencies, the social trends, the economic conditions, even the religious aspirations of the time.'

The problem of dress is thus not a minor matter for anyone who has the welfare of India's tribes at heart. Up till recently, many tribesmen had, and some still have, their own distinctive way of clothing themselves, and this is often artistic and well adapted to the conditions of their life. A very few prefer to wear skins and furs, though they all have a reserve of cloth to wear on occasion; others have a very simple dress, the men being content with a loincloth and the women with a skirt, leaving the upper part of the body bare. These usually have some kind of shawl for protection against the cold, and make ingenious rain-coats of grass. A third class has more elaborate clothing, such as may be found in Kameng, Siang and Lohit, while a fourth has begun to affect a fantastic medley of tribal and semi-civilized attire; a trilby hat perches above a splendid array of beads, a cast-off dinner jacket is worn above an apron adorned with cowries. And finally, there are a number of tribal people who have taken to full European dress — it is very rare to see one of them in a dhoti.

The advance of the Administration into NEFA has created a cultural ferment, and the people are on the move. Perhaps our greatest problem, and it is one which lays a very heavy load of responsibility on every officer, is to ensure that the move will be upward and not downward. Nowhere is this more necessary than in the field of dress.

We do not want to put the clock back or preserve NEFA as a sort of museum. But we do want the best for the people, and in this important matter, they should not be left without guidance. Otherwise, it will be in the shops that they will learn their lessons and the Marwari will be the Sartorial Adviser to the Administration. Tribal dress should not remain static; it should grow and develop, but on its own lines. This will not be done by putting everyone into shirts and shorts, blouses and frocks: that destroys tribal dress altogether. Nor will it be done by adding to the existing dress the cheapest and tawdriest singlets, blankets, plastic ornaments, sola topis and other products of the mills.

Fashion is Folly's child, and in an area where our policy is one of planned and scientific advance, we should not with-hold tactful and intelligent guidance. As the Prime Minister has said, 'There must be some check to prevent the degradation of public taste.'

Let us now consider, under a number of headings, the various aspects of tribal dress, and the possible consequences of the wrong kind of change. We will consider the subject in general first, and then see how it may be applied to NEFA.

Social and Political Aspects of Dress

Throughout the world clothes are used to proclaim social rank and status. There is a distinctive dress for royalty, at least on ceremonial occasions, a conventional dress for lawyers, doctors and clergy. The political use of clothes is illustrated by the distinctive uniform recently laid down by the Congress President for the use of Congressmen. A Congressman should wear a white cap, a shirt, pyjamas or a dhoti, and a pair of chappals, and should carry a leather bag.

Similarly in tribal Assam, dress is, in certain areas at least, carefully graded according to rank. A change of dress thus tends to disturb tribal organization and discipline.

The missionaries were not slow to recognise this. A Baptist missionary at the beginning of the century wrote: 'Amid these exhibitions of taste so degrading and repulsive we observe with encouragement and delight the slightest evidence of some innate refinement. . . A costume of jacket and body-cloth is now being adopted by many who have come under Christian influence, especially by pupils in the schools.' In recent years the adoption of some kind of Western dress is almost as inevitable a token of conversion as Bible-reading and singing hymns. In Manipur the missionaries have insisted on their converts abandoning their traditional way of dressing the hair.

An interesting parallel is found in the New Hebrides, of which Harrison has written: 'The shirt became the essential symbol of Christianity in the islands. The pastors made an absolute distinction between "native" and European clothing. A "native" could not be a Christian in his own clothes; no Christian woman could show her breasts, as every woman had always done before. Trousers and shirt were the entrance-marks to church service.' Christians were compelled to shave off their beards, which were regarded as a sign of heathenism. And one of the missionaries declared: 'When the native becomes a Christian, a great change comes over him — in his clothing, in his life, in his face.'

The danger of this adoption of western dress is that it not only makes boys and girls misfits in their own villages, but it creates a feeling of superiority towards India generally. Foreign dress creates a foreign outlook. In Manipur, for example, some of the Tangkhuls spoke to me derisively of 'the dhoti-civilization' in India. I was told in Tuensang by more than one Christian youth that 'what we want is American dress, language and way of life.' Our boys and girls, so strangely westernized, would not be happy even in the Assam Plains, where there is a simplicity of living and a beauty and innocence of dress that we are in real danger of losing in NEFA.

A change of dress often means a new psychology, a scorn of the traditions of one's tribe, a sense of being ashamed of it. This leads to a break-down of tribal discipline: a youth in smart English clothes and a sola topi will not obey his tribal chief, who looks so 'jungly' in his classic attire; girls in meretricious blouses and even trousers, with lipstick on their lips and phoney trinkets in their hair, are already showing signs of rebellion against the discipline of the community. A certain degree of rebellion is good and is a necessary stimulant to progress, but it is dangerous to foster a rapid break-down of tribal law and discipline. Social collapse may easily lead to moral degradation and political disturbance.

This does not happen where a tribe has had time to adjust itself to new conditions, and some of the most educated tribal people, who have gradually acclimatized themselves over a period of many years, are among those who are proudest of their race and its traditions.

The Aesthetic Importance of Dress

The aesthetic result of a change of dress is usually disastrous. Many of the NEFA tribes weave, and weave well, with patterns and colours that have evolved over a long period of years and which are almost always artistic, durable and appropriate. As Dr Hutton says: 'All Naga tribes have a most remarkable appreciation of the effective and picturesque in dress, and their use of colour is usually in extraordinary good taste and particularly well adapted to the surroundings in which it is displayed. The designs of their cloths are conspicuous for the right use of brilliant colours, while their ornaments of black and white hornbill feathers, cowries, ivory and scarlet hair seem peculiarly well fitted to the deep green or bluish background usually afforded by the well-wooded hills which are their home.' External influence throughout the tribal areas has done much to banish this beauty and the artistic sense has too often been stifled in 'the interests of a gloomy and puritanical view of life which is being imposed on them just as Europe is beginning to escape from its shackles.'

One of the greatest of the many crimes that 'civilization' has committed against the tribal people all over the world is to have made them ashamed of their own art and culture.

As long ago as 1901 Rabindranath Tagore foresaw the aesthetic impoverishment that would follow the adoption of European dress in India, and his essay *Nakaler Nakal* is so important and sensible that I will briefly summarize it. Tagore begins by quoting the saying that there is but one step from the sublime to the ridiculous. In Sanskrit rhetoric, he continues, '*adbhut rasa* expresses what sublimity does in English. But there are two varieties of *adbhut*, the one that causes wonderment and the other that provokes laughter.' He goes on to describe how on a short trip to Darjeeling, he encountered both these varieties of *adbhut* — 'on the one hand the divine Himalaya, and on the other the Bengali in English dress — the sublime and the ridiculous in close juxtaposition.'

Tagore does not, of course, think that English dress is in itself ridiculous, or even that the Bengali in English dress is necessarily ridiculous. But he does insist that the wrong kind of European dress on the wrong kind of Bengali, if not pathetic, is certainly ridiculous. 'The hat on his head, perhaps, is out of keeping with the dress he wears; perhaps he wears a collar but no tie; perhaps his coat is of a colour that would horrify an Englishman; or perhaps he comes out in what an Englishman would consider undress, fit only to be worn in one's bedroom. Why this unconscious clowning? If an Englishman were to go about in a Bengali locality in a dhoti — with the *kacha* in front and the *koncha* behind — he could not expect to win the respect of those who saw him. Our Bengali brother who visits the court of the King of the Mountains dressed in his clown's motley only spends his hard-earned money to provide free entertainment for his English spectators'.

Tagore thinks that the reason why so many poor people take to English dress is that it makes them superior to their neighbours, but he questions whether this really achieves its end. Most people are too poor to dress properly in foreign clothes.

'One or two jackdaws may be able to put on peacock's feathers becomingly, but the majority of them will never succeed in doing so, for they have no access to the society of peacocks. Under these circumstances, to save the entire jackdaw society from ridicule, the one or two successful imitators must resist the temptation of wearing their disguise. Otherwise the ludicrous spectacle of jackdaws flaunting their ill-assorted and ill-fitting borrowed plumes will be seen everywhere.

'There is no more abject spectacle than the Indian dressed in shabby and ill-fitting European clothes; he can never look so poor and lowly in Indian dress. One reason for this is that in European dress there is no simplicity; it involves much planning and effort.

'When poverty-stricken India stands up clothed in the ragged and cast-off clothes of England, what a grotesquely alien form her penury will take! What is only lamentable today will then become food for cruel laughter. The meagreness of dress that is today covered by a simple humility will then suffer ruthless exposure in the half-naked vulgarity of tattered coat and trousers.'

Tagore concludes that 'if we remember that a man does not derive his dignity from his clothes but rather lends dignity to them by wearing them, then we shall see that the wearing of coarse-spun *dhoti* and *chadar* is by no means a thing to be ashamed of. Vidyasagar, and not only Vidyasagar but scores of other great

Brahmin pandits, were incomparably nobler in character and dignity than any coat-clad England-returned person we know; and it is a matter of common knowledge that the great Brahmins who once brought India to the peak of civilization were scantily clad in the simplest dresses'. Tagore did not feel able to press for *dhotis* in offices, but he did urge some kind of Indian dress which would be natural and appropriate. I have no doubt whatever what his advice would have been, had he been presented with a choice between a Mishmi coat and a singlet; or a beautiful Phom or Chang *lengta* with its gleaming brass and a pair of shorts. Incidentally, I see no reason why the exiguous perineal band worn by some tribes should not be transformed into an ample and artistic apron such as is worn by the Sangtams and Semas. In Siang there are very fine such 'aprons' made of tiger or leopard skin. A new type of *lengta*, beautifully designed and woven in the CITCP at Mon, is becoming popular among the Konyaks.

But it is not only that a change of dress spoils the aesthetic appearance of the people; there is something more. For many tribes, dress and personal decoration is the one medium of art. A large part of their imagination, interest and creative ability is devoted to their own persons; much of their wit lies in their wardrobes. The Naga groups are good wood-carvers, and much of this carving is of ornaments to be worn on the body. Other tribes have no real art except the weaving of cloth, and the cane-work through which they make their remarkably fine hats. Many of the tribal boys and girls are expert in making ornaments out of simple and natural things.

A Konyak youth is himself a work of art. But take him to school, and at once he strips himself of all his glory, and in a few days this splendid boy, who formerly had the air of a prince, looks like a coolie.

Is this progress?

The Moral Influence of Dress

The effect of an alien type of dress on people accustomed to light and simple attire has been carefuly studied by Ehrenfels in his book on the Kadars of South India.

The first result is the creation of a sense of shame and

embarrassment. Ehrenfels describes how a Kadan woman, who normally goes about with breasts exposed, will, on the approach of a stranger, 'bow down and sit in a crouching position covering her breasts with crossed arms and spread palms.' 'The generally well-shaped, healthy breasts of Kadan women, once a matter of pride and a sign of health and fertility, have thus come to be considered by them as something to be ashamed of, almost as something that is repulsive and degrading.' He points out that this feeling has been created by the plainsmen who are 'in the habit of laughing ostentatiously and passing remarks.' Even little Kadan girls of five and six years have begun to 'imitate the humiliating gestures, covering their scarce discernible baby nipples with outspread palms, crouching and bowing down in a servile fashion as soon as an outsider appears.'

This has had its psychological effect. In the first place, it has made the Kadan woman servile instead of proud. 'The same person who looks dignified, free and self-confident in her healthy simplicity — well adapted to the climate and open-air work — becomes a caricature of dirt-covered, cringing servility. The dress-mania of modern civilization, Western and Oriental alike, demands its full share in sacrifice of human happiness and self-respect.'

Then, the Kadan woman, weary of crouching, has begun to buy brightly-coloured European blouses at fantastic prices, which she can ill afford. But the blouses are not sufficient to hide completely 'the indecent mammary appendages', and so she goes a step further and wears a singlet underneath the blouse. The introduction of the singlet into tropical countries has been 'to create an instrument of subtle self-torture for women as well as men.' It is uncomfortable; it is the most fruitful source of itch; and in the heat it clings unbearably to the body.

'Modern Kadan women quite naturally find it increasingly difficult to go to the jungle and dig for edible roots in the dusty ground, thereby spoiling their costly blouses and getting overheated in their thick singlets. To avoid both, they begin to sit at home. In the laziness and uniformity of this latest form of purdah, other new affectations are being adopted from the plains-people.' Heavy oiling and flattening of the naturally curled hair is one of them and this wastes much time.

This throws a new burden on the Kadan man who has to work harder to make up for his wife's laziness and to provide her with things she demands. If he does not provide them she will find someone who will. A shadow falls on the home. The husband begins to feel resentment at his wife; she is no longer his equal partner; she is now an economic liability. And hence clothes mean actually a lower position for women. 'From a free and equal partner in life's struggles and joys, the Kadan woman is gradually but steadily sliding into the position of: first a commodity, then a menial serf, and ultimately a drudge. Once an equal partner of men in the strenuous but healthy life of independent food-gatherers, she now becomes the slave of enslaved men, working in the iron grip of the new order which foreign clothing habits, economic pressure and direct propaganda are introducing into this originally bilateral society.'

I think that this elaborate analysis, which is supported by my own observations over a long period of years in Bastar and Orissa, deserves careful consideration.

Many years ago Bernard Shaw delivered a telling speech on the Sex Appeal of Clothes. He pointed out that there are two types of amateurs: 'One set seeks to minimise sex appeal by a maximum of clothing: the other seeks to maximise sex appeal by a minimum of clothing'. Both are completely and hopelessly wrong. 'If you want sex appeal raised to the utmost point, there is only one way of doing it, and that is by clothes. In hot climates the purpose of clothing must have been sex appeal and not protection from the inclemency of the weather, because in such places the weather tempts people to take off their clothes instead of to put them on.'

Bernard Shaw illustrated this point by a description of the Victorian woman. She was a masterpiece of sex appeal. 'She was sex appeal from the top of her head to the soles of her feet. She was clothed, of course, from head to foot; all clothes! Everything about her except her cheeks and her nose was a guilty secret, a thing you had to guess at. All young men and boys then thrilled with the magic and mystery of the invisible world under those clothes'. Shaw pointed out that on the other hand, 'those actresses of the French stage who made a speciality of sex appeal never undressed themselves in public. I do not know how many petticoats they wore; but at any rate instead of exposing their persons they just gave you a little glimpse of what looked like a dozen frilled pink petticoats round the ankles; and the effect was tremendous. The result was that the Victorian age was an exceedingly immoral age'.

Shaw spoke of the 'significant spread of nudism', especially in pre-war Austria, 'where you have clubs of people who have the extremely wholesome habit of meeting one another without anything on at all; for that gets rid of sex appeal altogether.' By contrast he found some of the churches in Italy full of notices ordering women to be fully clothed, 'all suggesting some impropriety or other which would never come into the head of a decent normal person if it were not officially placarded'. 'Every placard pointed out some particular aphrodisiac effect that would be produced on young men if women were not muffled up so that no one could see that they had bodies.' And he concluded his lecture with the words: 'I point no moral. I have simply given you the expert's practical directions. If you want sex appeal, clothes. If you want to minimise sex appeal, get rid of as many clothes as possible.'

It is interesting to find that Mahatma Gandhi took a rather similar view of clothes and nudity. When some of his followers came to him in South Africa and spoke of the evil custom of the Africans who went about unclad, he rebuked them, pointing out that the evil lay, not in the custom, but in the impure eye of the beholder. 'When a large society follows a particular custom, it is quite possible that the custom is harmless enough even if it seems highly improper to the members of another society. These Negroes have no time to be staring at one another . . . it is only vanity which makes us look on the Negroes as savages. They are not the barbarians we imagine them to be.'

And on another occasion Gandhiji said this: 'I believe that the ideal state of man is *digambara*. I hold the state of nakedness dear. Were I living in a forest, I would go without clothes. Nature has clothed mankind in skin . . . The loftiest beauty of man lies in his nudity.'

Generally speaking, the fewer clothes a tribe wears, the stronger is its sense of sexual morality, especially in relation to outsiders. This fact has been observed in many parts of the world, and I myself found it strikingly illustrated in the case of the Cabrais of French Togo, most of whom go completely naked and where there is a very high standard of morality indeed.

I have emphasized this, because some conventionally educated members of our staff, and even more their wives, are profoundly shocked when confronted with people who are scantily clad. This feeling of prudery, and the artificial attempts to clothe the people which it inspires, is wrong. It is probable that clothes will come everywhere, but let them come naturally: let the people make their own, in their own way, and because clothing is an art, not out of a sense of embarassment and shame.

We have another problem with regard to a change of dress. When a tribal girl in the interior attires herself in 'modern' fashion, especially if she goes in for gaudy and unfamiliar things, uses lip-stick and powder, puts on trousers, and does her hair differently, she is regarded as of loose character and is immediately exposed to temptations which normally might not come her way. Not only do tribal boys suppose her to be 'easy game', but subordinate officials and others quite naturally turn their attention towards any girl who looks accessible.

To my mind this is the most serious of all the effects of the 'modernization' of dress among girls, and it is a point which should be most carefully considered.

The Economics of Dress

The introduction of alien dress is bound to have a considerable effect on the economics of the people. Hitherto in many (though not all) areas the tribal women have done their own weaving. Where weaving was unknown, clothes of skin, grasses, bark and so on were worn. But the opening up of the country has brought the danger that the natural hand-weaving industry, which would have delighted the heart of Gandhiji, may die out in face of foreign competition. Once people find that they can buy cloth, and still more when cloth so bought is regarded as conferring a greater dignity and social status, they will cease to weave.

As they cease to weave they begin to send their money out of the village and almost always into the pockets of non-tribals. This makes them dependent on a class of adventurers who are the last persons whom one would choose to guide and lead the simple tribesmen.

A girl who comes down to Pasighat to sell some of her farm produce may in the evening attend a lantern lecture by the Medical

Officer on Improved Nutrition. He will urge her to buy eggs or milk for the nourishment of her child with the money she has just earned. But it is much more likely that she will purchase some gaudy bit of cloth for a blouse, some cosmetics or plastic ornaments — things that she does not need, that are inartistic and out of place — instead of using her money for the advantage of herself or her children.

Harrison described the subsidiary effects of 'Shortism' as follows: 'Economically the "mission natives" were thus firmly yoked to the trader, or to copra or sandalwood production, so that they might get clothes; they were supplied with the poorest clothes that rot quickly in this rotting climate; hygenically, clothes could not be kept clean within the tribal standard of living, so that skin disease, tuberculosis and parasites benefitted. Psychologically a new element of shame and secrecy was introduced into the open, balanced approach of the sexes'.

One of the chief reasons for our stress on the preservation of tribal dress in NEFA is, as I show later, an economic one, and we have already made progress in controlling imports, guiding expenditure and promoting the hand-loom industry, all of which saves the people money or at least keeps it in their own area. Swadeshi is as important for NEFA today as it once was for the whole of India.

Dress and Health

The adverse effect of unfamiliar and unsuitable dress on the health of primitive people has been reported by observers from all over the world, and I can only refer to a few of even the Indian authorities on the subject. Thus, Mr J. P. Mills, who had a wide experience of the Assam tribes, observes in a passage which I have slightly modified:

> 'Foreign clothes are dangerous from more than one point of view. They undoubtedly spread disease. A tribal who wears them does not always change them when he should; probably he has no others to put on. A man will arrive at the top of a hill streaming with perspiration and then take his coat off to get cool. The wearing of foreign clothes has, in my opinion, contributed to the spread of pulmonary disease in the hills. Secondly, they are entirely

unfitted to the tribal mode of life. Long skirts for women are not suitable garments for weeding in rice drenched with rain. A dhoti or shorts are possibly worse. The close-fitting bodices for women and shirts for men are positively dangerous in a climate where workers are soaked daily with rain or perspiration'.

A book which should be studied by all administrators of tribal areas is *Essays on the Depopulation of Melanesia*, edited by the famous physician and psychologist, W. H. R. Rivers. The essays are contributed by a number of scientists and, though they disagree on some matters, they are unanimous on the subject of clothes. All of them include the wearing of European clothes as one, if not the most important, of the principal factors in bringing about the spread of lung diseases and the consequent decimation of those who have adopted them. In Melanesia, not only lung diseases, but dysentery, itch and yaws were all propagated by the foolish habit of wearing English clothes quite unsuited to the temperament and environment of the wearers. 'Everything should be done to keep the people natural and unaffected, and to prevent a false modesty and artificiality. It cannot be said that modesty is encouraged by the wearing of clothes; perhaps even the reverse is true. . . One of the most pathetic contrasts in the islands is the lithe and glossy skin of the healthy islander and the dirty, over-dressed Melanesian masquerading as a white man'. In Melanesia even the missionaries now, as well as administrators, recommend a return to the Fijian or Samoan *lavalava*, a palm-leaf petticoat, and in this book it is a missionary who points out that the very infants suffer from the clothes-wearing habits of their mothers, who must carry them on their backs on wet days with sodden cloth on all sides of them instead of, at worst, on the outside only.

Harrison, whom I have already quoted, says of 'Shortism' in the New Hebrides that skin-disease, tuberculosis and parasites are the chief beneficiaries of the policy of more clothes. Grigson points out that in Bastar it is because the Hill Marias wear so little that they are 'far freer from scabies, itch and ringworm than the tribesmen of the plains, who more and more are imitating Hindu clothes, but are too poor to afford either much clothing or spare suits. At the numerous State dispensaries these are the commonest complaints and treatment is useless because the patients will not leave off the dirty infected clothing.'

There has recently been an interesting discussion of this subject in *Time* magazine. Professor Huntington of Yale has argued that the highest forms of civilization must develop in temperate climates. If a country is too cold, its people have to struggle too hard just to stay alive. If it is too hot, they relax into a slow-moving lassitude. In reply to this, an anthropologist, Dr Wulsin of Massachusetts, has declared that it is neither the heat nor the humidity, but over-dressing that robs tropical residents of their energy. The human body has its own methods of keeping itself at the proper temperature. Heat escapes by radiation, by convection and reduction to the air and through the cooling effect of evaporation. When it does not escape fast enough, the temperature of the internal organs rises. The heart pumps harder to carry more blood to the surface. Sometimes so much blood is needed for carrying heat that not enough remains to make the body work properly.

In warm weather or during exercise the evaporation of sweat does most of the final cooling. But the body cannot produce an unlimited amount of sweat, and if it is forced to do so, there are various ill effects. So the natural reaction of the overheated human is to sit still until his temperature falls. In the long run this defensive lassitude lowers the cultural level.

Dr Wulsin describes experiments on how clothes hamper the body in keeping itself cool. They act as insulators, checking heat-loss by radiation. More important, they create near the skin a layer of hot, moisture-saturated air. Sweat cannot evaporate until it has soaked through the clothing, and then its cooling effect is largely wasted. Europeans in the tropics who wear helmets and heavy clothing to keep off the sun make a great mistake. The less they wear the better off they will be.

The alleged inferiority of hot-country civilizations is a myth. The ancient cultures of Egypt, Mesopotamia, of the Mayans and Indonesia were not developed under climates cooler than they are today. There has been no significant changes in climate — except in the climate next to the people's skins.

'In the old days, people in the tropics wore little clothing, usually nothing above the waist. Now tropical people, of European culture, clinging to European customs, go clothed as if they were dressing for a chilly British spring. The natural result is lassitude and a lowered cultural level.' The Balinese, despite the warm humidity of their climate, have maintained for centuries a vigorous art and culture, partly because they have had the sense not to wear too much. Today, under the influence of an imported puritanism, they are being forced to cover themselves and are in danger of falling into lassitude and decay.

Equally, scientific observers point out that clothing is not necessary as a defence against the cold. The insular group known as Tierra del Fuego, at the southern extremity of South America, is afflicted by a bitterly cold and raw climate. Yet the majority of the inhabitants go naked or almost naked, and are impervious to cold. Some of the NEFA tribes which are most indifferent to clothes live on the tops of hills. The human body is admirably adjusted, in its natural state, to varying climates. Once, however, it takes to clothes, it needs more and more of them.

Investigations among the Konyaks of the Tuensang Division have shown that in the interior villages, where the people like to wear very little (though they all have clothes to wear on occasion), there are few cases of skin infection, but villages near the sub-divisional headquarters at Mon and the plains of Assam, where the people have taken to wearing more clothes, are seriously affected by scabies and other skin diseases. One of our doctors has written: 'People in these parts have taken to wearing old, dirty rags which are never cleaned. Some of them were soaked and stinking with pus but still we found the patients unwilling to part with them. I have never seen such severe skin infections. In some cases it took hours to clean all the pus and scabs before we could apply the medicine. There were instances where there was hardly any patch of skin free from the infection. It is good to wear clothes when one can afford to keep them clean. Otherwise it is better and healthier to remain naked. I would certainly choose to remain naked all my life than be clothed and suffer from the dreadful infections I saw during my visits to some of these villages.'

This increase in skin infections appears to have been very rapid, A.S.C. porters, who are issued with clothes by the Administration, being specially afflicted with scabies.

It is obviously true that 'the sight of a healthy skin is more decent than that of a dirty shirt.'

The Situation in NEFA

That great authority on the social significance of clothes, taste and fashion, James Laver, has proposed three fundamental principles of clothing: hierarchy, utility and attractiveness.

As elsewhere in the world, dress in NEFA often indicates a person's status in the social hierarchy. In the Naga group of tribes, a Chief wears one kind of attire, a commoner another. A successful warrior has privileges denied to others. A Sherdukpen Thong can put on ceremonial dress allowed only to the aristocracy. Everywhere there are special ornaments worn only by leading men. We have recognized this by providing headmen and interpreters with red coats or blankets, which are not worn by others. Even the style of hair-dressing may indicate status. An Ang's daughter among the Konyaks wears her hair long; others must cut it short. And the dress of women often suggests their domestic position. A married woman has different ornaments and clothes from an unmarried girl; among the Sherdukpens, girls of different ages must do their hair in different styles.

Much of the tribal dress-fashions in NEFA depend on the principle of utility. The Monpas and Sherdukpens, even the women, wear long sleeves and pyjamas to protect them against the bites of dim-dam flies. The warlike Tagins and northern Gallongs dress, when they bother to dress at all, in an armour of leather and their hats are strong and heavy to ward off the blows of enemies. Women accustomed to work in the fields wear short skirts, for long and clinging garments would impede the free use of their limbs.

The task of axe-cultivation is a very dirty one, for the people have to labour on hillsides covered with wood-ash; this is one of the reasons why so many of them prefer to go lightly clad when working, with only a small cloth round the loins. This is a sensible custom for those who do not have or cannot afford soap and for those who live in elevated villages where there is little water.

The attractiveness of tribal dress in NEFA varies greatly from place to place. At its best it has charm, variety and colour. To paraphrase Addison we may say that there is not so variable a thing in Nature as a Naga's head-dress. It would be hard to find a more splendid sight than a young Konyak 'apparelled like the spring' with his gay head-gear, the shining ornaments on his chest, his armlets. The dancing-dress of the Khienmungans is magnificent, and indeed throughout Tuensang the colour and gaiety of the genuine tribal attire is singularly attractive.

This is less so in Tirap, where the Noctes, for example, have long since lost the art of weaving before the competition of cheap mill-cloth from the plains, though we are now reviving it through the CITPC's. Many of the Mishmis have finely woven and pleasing cloth, and the best Adi coats and skirts are genuine works of art.

Some of the people of northern Subansiri, again, wear attractive brick-red garments purchased from Tibet — and indeed the Tibetan influence in the northern areas of Siang and Kameng is very beneficial in the realm of clothes. The Apa Tanis weave cloth in subdued but tasteful colours and this cloth is still purchased by the Daflas and Hill Miris. On the whole, however, the dress of the Daflas and Hill Miris is not colourful, though the hats of the men are among the most charming in NEFA.

We must remember, of course, that tribal values in dress are not our values. An Englishman may feel embarrassed if he fails to carry gloves on a formal occasion. If he forgets to wear a tie with a dinner-jacket he will feel positively naked. On the other hand, a Phom or Chang may be perfectly happy with nothing covering his buttocks, yet he will be awkward if he has omitted to put on his ivory armlets. A tribal girl may feel more embarrassed if she has no bracelets (for this may suggest that she is a widow) than if she has no blouse. We must, not, therefore, judge tribal standards of dress by our own; above all, we must not apply our ideas of 'decency' to people who have lived for generations in an innocence which we have never known. 'Fashion is what I wear myself. The unfashionable is what other people wear.'

Three Important Points

In all our efforts to preserve the colour and beauty of the best elements of tribal dress and ornamentation, it is necessary to bear in mind three important points.

The first is that our approach to the whole subject must be a dynamic one: we must keep on the move. It is no use merely bewailing the passing of picturesque old fashions and trying to freeze existing custom as it is. Change will come everywhere, even in the remotest places, and our task is not to check it but to guide it. If a culture does not evolve, it dies. Our aim should to bring *more* colour, *more* beauty into NEFA, not to be content with the often drab and sometimes rather ludicrous clothing that exists at present. As the people become 'civilized' we should help them to evolve a form of dress which will remain truly tribal, but more artistic, more attractive and more appropriate.

I cannot myself believe that there is any real reason why NEFA should lose its distinctiveness, its beauty and its variety. It will be a tragedy if it does.

The example of the people of the Wahgi Valley of central New Guinea suggests that progress does not necessarily mean a loss of beauty. 'These people,' says Colin Simpson in his fascinating book *Adam in Plumes*, 'are more colourful in their adornment now than they were before they had contact with civilization twenty years ago. . . This is so against the rule that civilization is the bleach and solvent of tribal colour that the circumstances may well be unique; but it is quite explicable.' Colin Simpson goes on to describe how traders brought into the country great quantities of mother-of-pearl shell, which was the basis of ornamentation but which previously the people had found difficult to obtain; they imported bird-of-paradise plumes from other areas; they supplied a better and more colourful type of pigment for painting the face.

'That they remain as decorative as they are is not entirely due to the fact that civilization has touched them only lightly; the Administration has, more or less, set its face against the introduction of singlets to the men, and nowhere has that dreadful early missionary shroud, the Mother Hubbard smock, been inflicted on the women.'

A two-fold policy, of providing the right kind of things in the shops and of checking the import of the wrong kind of things has thus had an excellent result.

The second point is that we must recognise the fact that a certain number of our boys and girls will become largely 'modernized', at all events in such externals as dress and general style of living. These will be the Political Officers, the politicians, the doctors and lawyers, the engineers of the future. We may hope that they will not grow up to be ashamed of their race and with a scorn of the simple ways and beliefs of their fathers, but they are — in the context of modern India which so curiously prefers the drabness of western attire to its own traditions — almost certain to give up most of their own sartorial fashions. This need not necessarily be true of girls, for if we can develop the hand-loom industry as we hope to do, NEFA girls of the future will (like Lushai girls) weave beautiful cloth, developed from the old designs, which they will wear in their own fashion. Some of the older ornaments too have a beauty that the most sophisticated young women need not despise.

The third point is that the problem of dress is only part of a much bigger problem, the problem of detribalization as a whole. It is no good trying to preserve and develop tribal dress unless we are going to do the same for tribal institutions, tribal religion and tribal dance, song and art. The same attitude of respect for all good tribal things must run through every aspect of life. To this I shall return in the next chapter.

The final word was said by Tagore in the article already quoted. 'Is change,' he asks, 'to be ruled out altogether in the sphere of dress? Change is bound to come, but it follows the law of necessity, not the law of imitation; because imitation is very often opposed to necessity, it is not conducive to health or happiness or peace. It is out of keeping with its surroundings, it has to be achieved by effort and maintained with difficulty.'

Tagore gives sound advice to anyone who wants to change his way of dress. 'See that it harmonizes with your way of life, your surroundings and the traditions of your country. Do not be led unthinkingly into imitation of what goes against the history, the sentiments and the taste of your own people. How far change can go without becoming imitation, it is difficult to say with certainly. But in general it may be said that it is assimilation where the thing borrowed harmonizes with the things one has already, and that it is imitation where the thing adopted strikes one as incongruous.'

Part Four

PSYCHOLOGICAL AIMS IN NEFA

The Danger of Creating an Inferiority Complex

In the book, *Adam in Plumes*, already quoted, Colin Simpson makes an estimate of the effect of civilization on primitive communities: 'Pride was going, pride in creation. And that I feel is the depressing thing that always follows on foreign contact: the tribal feels that he and his works are, by comparison, second-rate. We bring him a new world of ideas, a new freedom from fear, new foods to grow, new sensations to enjoy, new ways to live more healthily; there is a big credit side. And on the debit side we bring him an inferiority complex.'

An inferiority complex is a dangerous thing; it poisons the sources of individual happiness, making a man abnormally sensitive, bitter and resentful. It is destructive of art and culture, causing people to despise their own ideas and customs and to regard their own creations as inferior. It can disturb the political relations between two communities, and in the tribal areas can ruin the relations between the hill people and the outside world.

In NEFA there are already signs that there is a danger of creating this sense of cultural and political inferiority. 'I am so ashamed of being a Konyak', exclaimed a Konyak boy. One of the leading tribal interpreters in Tirap told me that he felt so ashamed of being a Naga that whenever he went down to the plains and mixed with other people, he described himself as Chinese. There was reason, in his opinion, for doing so. The difference in the way he was treated, he said, was remarkable; at once he was given the respect and position that was denied to him as a NEFA tribesman.

One of our Adi interpreters who went to Delhi told me that he had been rebuked there by a leading politician for appearing before him in a loin-cloth. 'When this great man said this to me,' said the Adi, 'I felt that I was not a human being at all. I felt that I was a monkey and my proper place was among the trees.' An Apa Tani used very similar words in describing his reactions to the magnificence of the buildings and personalities of the capital; 'they made me feel like a monkey of the hills.'

The inferiority complex is mainly developed in the educated and those who come into close contact with officers of the Administration and, even more, with the people of the plains. It is expressed in an exaggerated sensitiveness and a readiness to resent a slight; in a belief that all outsiders, and even our own officers, look down on them and despise their culture; and paradoxically in a desire to eliminate anything 'tribal' from their lives. Thus we have a growing attachment to European dress among the educated, the use of the sola topi which in villages is still the symbol of a higher culture, sometimes a refusal to join in the dances or songs, sometimes even the adoption of another religion. The inferiority complex is the knife that severs the link that binds the people to their past; it is the sponge that wipes out a thousand years of history. If it continues to develop in NEFA it will destroy tribal art, culture and religion, for the people will not hold to something of which they have become ashamed; and it will lead to a wholesale collapse of tribal moral sanctions and of the social organization which at present holds the tribes together.

A distinguished missionary, writing in the *Geographical Magazine* of the situation in the Gold Coast, has said: 'The source of much of the desperate frustration of Africa is a fundamental lack of faith in the contribution of the coloured people, not only on the part of the white folk, but among the Africans themselves. The fantastic technical success of modern, Western, man seems so to dazzle the eyes of black and white alike that the European easily assumes a similar superiority in all other spheres of life, and the African, bedevilled with self-mistrust, seeks only to play a resentful second fiddle to the white man's tune. Whereby the world is much the poorer. For the tune we play is largely materialist, the atonal music of extreme individualism; it is the African contribution, if we would only hear it, which might restore to us a sense of the unseen world, and the wisdom of a richer communal relationship.'

Substitute 'NEFA tribal' for African and ourselves for 'European' in the above passage, and it will serve as a serious warning of what might happen in NEFA.

The fundamental objection to missionary effort, of whatever religion, or even of social reform work, is that it greatly increases self-distrust. By pouring scorn on tribal beliefs and customs, it creates a sense of inferiority even among those who refuse to become converts. To be told constantly that whatever is tribal is evil, or at least 'backward', produces a frustration and despair which may have unexpected political consequences, as among the Mau-Mau. For this reason, the use of the word 'samsari' for non-Christians in Tuensang is to be deprecated. And this leads to a second danger, the danger of detribalization.

Detribalization of a kind and to some degree, as I have already pointed out, will be inevitable in certain cases. The boy who goes to the University, who will be trained up to be a future Superintending Engineer, Director of Health Services, or Deputy Adviser, will certainly shed many of his tribal characteristics; he will wear whatever dress convention dictates at the time and live in the same style as officers from other parts of India. And this will do no harm, provided such detribalization has come about naturally and not as a reaction against a despised past or as a symptom of an inferiority complex.

But detribalization among the ordinary villagers who are continuing to live their own lives in their own homes is destructive of art and culture and may easily lead to political discontent. A boy or girl who has adopted western dress, learnt to despise the laws and rulers of his tribe, acquired a taste for 'modern' luxuries, finds life in an interior village intolerable. Caught between two worlds, at home in neither, he rebels culturally against the one and politically against the other.

What causes this inferiority complex? The first and perhaps the chief reason for it is simply that we, the outside people, are what we are. With the best will in the world, we are different and because we are different we are regarded as superior. There are a great many of us, and the more efficient we are, the more we develop our technological superiority, our military or semi-military power and our rapid advance, the more we tend to overwhelm the people of the hills. Lafcadio Hearn used to talk of the danger of exterminating other races 'merely by *overliving* them — by monopolizing and absorbing, almost without conscious effort, everything necessary to their happiness.'

This is true even of the best and most sympathetic officers. It becomes, of course, far worse when officers regard themselves as superior or as benefactors, when they laugh at tribal customs and ideas, when by failing to learn the local language they give the impression that it is not worth learning.

Our own lack of adjustment to local conditicns materially contributes to this. It has been said of a tribal house that it seems to grow out of the landscape. Of how many of our officers, or their wives, their dress, their houses, could it be said that they grow out.of the landscape? Too much of our life is different, alien, contrasted; we do not fit into the picture. The ultimate result of this may be to create a profound sense of inferiority among the people or at the least to produce a small class of tribal 'sahibs' who will imitate us and alienate themselves from their own civilization. But the mass of the folk are not likely to do this and they may resent both the detribalized, who elsewhere have often taken the lead in exploiting their poorer and simpler brethren, and our own unfamiliar presence.

The Example of Tawang

As an example of how we are trying to remedy what is clearly a grave defect, I will take the situation in Tawang.

Elsewhere we have the difficult, indeed vexatious, puzzle of the impact of the Atomic Age on a Stone Age people. But here we have the conflict between two civilizations, one of which is indeed immensely superior in technological achievement, while the other is equally distinguished by spiritual faith, by simple dignity, by compassionate goodness. I do not want to suggest that the culture of Tawang is above the best and finest culture of the modern world. But in many ways it is above the kind of culture that we are able to introduce within its boundaries.

For here are people, many of whom are great gentlemen, whose way of life is higher than that of the majority of our staff, who live better than all but the most senior of our officers — better housed, better and more appropriately clad, who are more reflective, more sensitive to aesthetic values, of more elevated manners.

Before going into such an area the ideal would have been to have given a specially selected staff at least a year's training, during which they would have mastered the local language, made a careful study of Buddhism and generally adjusted themselves to a new world of ideas. At th: same time, we would have been able to have put up buildings of dignity and suited both to the climate and to the general demands of the situation.

This was obviously impossible, for we had to go there in a hurry and the result has been that some of our establishments are alien and a little shabby compared to their's. Across the border also the Tibetan officials look much more in the picture than our's. They wear the same kind of dress and live in the same kind of house as the Monpas, and they carefully observe the local rules of precedence, which are important in an area where a person's significance is judged by the clothes he wears, the horse he rides and the kind of house he lives in.

Now, however, that we have had time to examine the situation and think things out, we are trying to remedy this. We hope, for example, to put up our official buildings in the local style, for the Monpa stone houses are not only well adjusted to the climate but are dignified and pleasant to live in. We have suggested to our officers that they might wear the local dress and in fact some of them are already doing so, though we have not, of course, insisted on this. We do insist, however, on them all learning as quickly as possible the local language. We are asking them to make a study of Buddhism so that they will not make mistakes out of ignorance, but on the other hand will approach the people with greater respect.

We are also exploring a proposal to work through the local monasteries in this area. At Dirang Dzong, there is a fine building, the Dzong, which at present is lying vacant and which, after being modernized and improved, would make an excellent Middle School. At Rupa and Shergaon, it might be possible to utilise the Gompas as our schools in the same way as is done in Sikkim, Ceylon and Thailand. In Tawang itself, the monastery already has a training establishment.

This might be described as a combination of an old-fashioned Cathedral School and a Basic Education Centre. A large number of boys come to the monastery to be trained, but in actual practice many of them marry and settle down to lay-life after a time. These boys are attached in groups to the senior Lamas who act as tutors. Some of the boys study in the library, others look after the ponies, cook in the kitchen, practise agriculture, care for the cattle, while yet others are trained in dancing, art-work and even printing. They work in the library in an atmosphere of art, religion and learning: the walls are painted with pictures and hung with scrolls. The boys sit on the floor on cushions covered with decorated mats and read on little tables placed in front of them. The atmosphere is almost that of one of the older European Universities or, as I have said, of a Cathedral School. But there is also the 'Basic' side: the boys get training in hygiene, the dignity of manual work and learn fundamental lessons of discipline, obedience and religious faith which remain with them all their lives.

We hope, provided the Lamas are willing, to work *through* this ancient and important institution; not to run a rival school, but to use the existing monastic school by enlarging its academic scope and opening its doors to the laity. Such an alliance will be of advantage to the monastery, where the education is along old-fashioned and restricted lines, as well as to our own activities which will thus be harmonized and adapted to a fine tradition.

To such areas, on the very borders of the country, we must bring the message that (in words attributed to the Lord Buddha himself) 'colourful and rich is India, lovable and charming is the life of men.'

Techniques of Adaptation

It should be comparatively easy to make the necessary readjustments in western Kameng: it will be more difficult elsewhere: it may even be impossible in, say, northern Subansiri.

But everywhere we are trying to modify the sharp contrasts and contradictions between official and tribal life — and we are doing this over a very wide field, in education, architecture, dress, language, even medicine.

The first and most important technique of adaptation, of course, applies to our own minds and hearts. A great deal has been written on the subject of the right approach to the tribal people and I have little to add here, except perhaps to say that it all sounds wonderful on paper but is by no means easy to carry out in practice. I have heard an officer declare that he is 'one with the tribals', that they are his brothers, and that he loves them as if they were members of his own family. Yet when it came to his arranging a Community Feast, I noticed that the higher officers were given chairs or at least good carpets to sit on and all sat together; that school-teachers, instead of sitting with their children, collected in a little group by themselves; that the tribal Chiefs and others were put together on inferior carpets, with inferior plates or dishes; and that the general public and children messed in somehow on the outskirts. I do not say this happens often, but it does sometimes happen and is hardly a symbol of human brotherhood.

I once attended a party, not I am happy to say in NEFA, where two kinds of *pan* were provided; the better quality was handed to the officials and their wives, the inferior quality to the tribal guests.

Someone once said to me that: 'The entire policy of the Prime Minister with regard to the tribal people of India may be summed up in one word — Humility'. I believe that this is true. Humility has been the dominant virtue of the most successful administrators of tribal areas throughout the world.

Humility is not a popular virtue and is not generally supposed to pay a very high dividend; it can, if insincere, be one of the most obnoxious of human characteristics. But if it is sincere, it will enable us to approach our task without fear of failure, save us from countless mistakes, and win us the true affection of many tribal friends.

In 1869, T. H. Lewin, a British soldier, who was entrusted with the administration of the Lushai Hills and became very popular there for his wise and friendly administration, made a remarkable statement which anticipated the attitude and policy of modern India towards the tribes.

'Let us not govern these hills for ourselves, but administer the country for the well-being and happiness of the people dwelling therein. What is wanted here is not measures, but a man. Place over them an officer gifted with the power of rule, not a mere cog in the great wheel of government, but one tolerant of the failings of his fellow-creatures and yet prompt to see and recognize in them the touch of nature that makes the whole world kin, apt to enter into new trains of thought and to modify and adopt ideas, but cautious in offending national prejudice. Under a guidance like this, let the people by slow degrees civilize themselves. With education open to them and yet moving under their own laws and customs, they will turn out not debased and miniature epitomes of Englishmen, but a new and noble type of God's creatures.'

It is important to watch the way we talk. We have already built up a tradition about this, and it is almost possible to recognise a NEFA officer by the kind of words and expressions he uses. In NEFA, for example, we do not use the word 'backward' to describe the people. We have come to see that its use is inconsistent with the attitude we have adopted, for it suggests that we are modern and advanced and our tribal friends are behind us. It implies a value-judgement, which the conscience of the world may yet reverse. For who is really backward — the honest peasant working in simplicity and truth among the hills, or the representative of modern progress embroiled in the mad race for power and wealth, the symbol of whose achievement is the hydrogen bomb?

The word 'uplift' too has similar connotations; it is a patronizing word, a benefactor's word, suggesting that we are stooping down to raise up those who are sunk in the mire of ignorance and sin. But we are not in NEFA as patrons and reformers. The only thing to which the word 'uplift' should be applied is a brassiere.

Other words to be avoided are 'betterment' and 'reform'. I once heard someone say that 'we must come down to the level of the tribals if we want to understand them'. It was the NEFA ideal that the speaker had not understood.

The tribal people are very sensitive to anything that savours of condescension, and while using the right words will not cure us of the outlook of the patron or benefactor, it is a help towards gaining a proper approach.

Language

Of highest importance is the learning of the local languages. A knowledge of the language is the window by which we see into the tribal mind; it is the door through which we shall most readily receive affection and co-operation. In former days, the most popular and useful officers were, almost without exception, those who could talk to the people in their own tongue. Reliance on interpreters has many disadvantages. A clever Kakati or Dobashi can lead an officer up the garden path; he can twist affairs to his own advantage or that of his own clan, village or tribe; in some places a cause of resentment and suspicion of the Administration is the feeling that officers allow themselves to be unduly swayed or even misrepresented by their interpreters.

And even as a cure for the feeling of inferiority, this is an essential matter. The tribal folk of Assam are intensely proud of their languages; the Khasis, for example, who have in the course of the past century changed their way of life in many respects, cling enthusiastically to the Khasi language. I know one fine Khasi scholar who refuses to write his books in any other tongue. When a man sees that the officers sent to work for him do not apparently think it worth their while to learn his language, it creates a feeling of depression, and stresses the so easily-created feeling that he belongs to an inferior race. On the other hand, when an officer approaches him with speech that he can understand, he is encouraged, excited and inspired with a pride in this essential element of his own culture.

For these and other reasons, the Administration has given top priority to the learning of the tribal languages.

We hope to build up gradually a whole literature for the people. This will first consist of books containing their own traditions, stories of their origins and migrations, songs and folk-tales. Later, we may well translate certain appropriate books. The people get a great kick out of possessing and being able to read even a little book of songs, and when such books are in their own tongue that pride will be all the stronger.

Education[1]

How does all this apply to the field of education?

The aim of education of NEFA is bound to be twofold, and the emphasis in these two aspects will obviously be somewhat different. We have first to discover and develop boys and girls of exceptional promise, and train them up to the highest standard possible so that they can in time take their place as leaders and administrators of their own people. But this can only apply to a very small proportion of the total population; for the great mass of the tribesmen, who will remain peasants, a very simple and elementary type of education is required and we hope that this will be supplied by Basic, suitably adjusted to tribal needs.

[1] This is not a discussion of Education in general, but of only one aspect of it.

But in both cases it is essential to guard against the dangers of detribalization. Hitherto our schools and our teachers have been such as to increase the dangers rather than to cure them. In the past there was little attempt at a serious adaptation to tribal life or at giving it any kind of tribal flavour. The style of the buildings, the dress alike of teachers and taught, the charts and pictures on the walls, the medium of instruction, the games were all alien to the local scene. The result was that instead of appearing as a natural function of village life, the school was something apart, even hostile to tribal tradition. There was nothing in our schools to foster a boy's pride in the institutions of his tribe, everything to make him ashamed of them. Although we often speak of a special education for NEFA, there has in fact been little to distinguish our schools from the conventional schools of the plains.

This state of things is a heritage of the past and today we are working hard to remedy it. In the first place, we are insisting that our school teachers should learn to give instruction in the local language as soon as possible and rules have been made that if they cannot pass an examination within a certain time, their increments will be withheld. We are also preparing text-books composed with special reference to local conditions and in the local dialects. Alphabet-charts are being made with illustrations which have an appropriate tribal background and these will take the place of the inartistic foreign charts and pictures which are at present displayed. Research has been made in tribal games and an illustrated booklet will soon be ready which will, we hope, encourage the playing of these games, some of which are very good, along with such new diversions as football and volley-ball. Gradually as we are able to produce a literature based on the traditions, stories and songs of the people in their own language, their minds will grow resistant to external depressing influences.

As we try to adjust our education to tribal life as a whole, our schools will cease to be places where the children lose their pride in being tribal, learn to despise their own religion, and forget their own traditions, their dances, their songs and their art.

An interesting example of how this has been achieved elsewhere is found in an account (by Prem Bhatia) of the Prime Minister's visit to the Central Institute for National Minorities at Peking. Here are nearly two thousand students, representing more than forty minorities, including many from Tibet, Sinkiang and Mongolia. 'The intention is to give the national minorities facilities to get together in a common field of instruction, at the same time retaining their separate national entities and characteristics. No attempt is made to iron out their national personalities. During our visit to classrooms we saw male Tibetan students dressed in their national costumes, complete with felt hats, which they wore during their lessons. Boys and girls from Singkiang retained their colourful dresses. There is a small but beautiful museum of representative arts and crafts and of costumes to familiarize each minority with the customs and habits of the others . . . The Prime Minister seemed charmed by the feast of colour and healthy variety.'

The transformation of the existing schools with their town-made syllabus and artificial urban approach by a modified Basic programme should make a great difference in relating them to the local economy and the actual life of the villages.

It is most important that the people should not feel that a school is something imposed by and belonging to Government but should really feel that it is their own institution, in the running of which they can take a part, and for which they are responsible. As we make the externals of the schools also more akin to the actual life of the people, this will become possible.

We have plans for using the existing institutions, such as the Gompas in the Buddhist areas, the morungs in Tuensang and Tirap and the boys' dormitories in Siang; if we can work through these, instead of in rivalry to them, not only will our schools be more attractive but many psychological complexes will be resolved.

At one time, teachers insisted on children changing their dress, removed their ornaments and even took the flowers out of their hair. Today, while allowing entire freedom to any boy or girl who wishes to change his way of dress, we are tactfully suggesting that there is nothing to be ashamed of in, for example, a good Mishmi or Adi coat or a Naga shawl. Considerable progress has already been made. Last year I found many of the boys at Rupa looking clownish in a strange medley of tribal and western fashions; this year everyone of the Sherdukpen boys was charming in his hat of yak's hair and his coat and sash.

In the Mishmi schools boys are of their own accord resuming their traditional attire. Girls of the Weaving Schools at Pasighat and Along, who had taken to dressing entirely in mill-cloth, now wear the beautiful Gallong or Padam-Minyong skirts and simple hand-woven blouses.

For the Pasighat High School, an excellent blazer has been designed. It is based on the Adi coat and is hand-woven on the Adi loom, but it is better tailored, the sleeves have been made longer, it has a collar, buttons and two pockets. It remains fully tribal, but is at the same time adapted to school needs. Similar coats, based on local designs, are being made for schools throughout the Agency.

We are also trying to promote good shorts of dark red, green or black colour with a stripe of tribal pattern down the side, instead of the conventional khaki, which does not match the colours of the coats or shawls.

Throughout NEFA, there is great variety in the style of dressing the hair by boys and girls, men and women. The Tangsas of Tirap do their hair in a knot on the top of the head, while their neighbours the Noctes do it in a style similar to that of the Vaishnavas of the plains. In Lohit, the Idu Mishmis cut their hair short while the Taraon Mishmis keep it long. In Siang, the Minyongs and Padams cut the hair short and the Gallongs, Bokars, Boris and other tribes allow it to grow.

There is indeed a very great variety of custom in dress and hair-style throughout India. For example, one of the most progressive communities, the Sikhs, are strongly attached to the traditional method of allowing their hair to grow long. The South Indian Brahmin may shave his head completely, while yet others do their hair in European style. The same applies to women and girls. Some of them cut their hair short: others tie it in a plait hanging down the back: others again roll it into a bun at the back of the head and so on.

In the past, there was a tendency on the part of some of our officers, and specially the school-teachers (no doubt due to ignorance), to persuade the people to change their hair-style.

The Administration has pointed out that this amounts to imposition and is, therefore, against our policy. At the same time it has emphasized that:

'We must not prevent a school boy or indeed anybody else from doing his hair in a style he pleases. Equally, however, we should not in any way suggest to him that there is something backward or uncivilized in his own traditional method. As a matter of fact all our officials and particularly school-teachers should always bear in mind our policy of creating an atmosphere of respect for tribal culture and the tribal way of doing things.

'To summarize, we are not to interfere if any boy or girl wishes to change his habit, but we should create an atmosphere in which the tribal people will not be ashamed to follow their own customs.'

These may seem to be small matters, yet taken together the total impact is considerable, and I have no doubt that as they are implemented, and self-confidence and pride is restored, the sense of inferiority will disappear.

At the same time, we need to be careful and selective in our educational policy. Mere numbers are no indication of success or lack of numbers of failure.

'It would be barbarous', said Rousseau, 'to twist a child's nature and kill his joy in preparing him for a future which may not be his.' It would be well to bear in mind the warning of the author of the note on Madhya Pradesh from which I have already quoted. Cultural penetration through education, he says, may have the effect of disturbing too rapidly a traditional society. The breaking of tribal loyalties leads to 'bewilderment, followed by disillusion, inevitably followed by social degeneration and crime.' A race of clerks is created, 'to which a large part of the recipients of this education are unfit to belong, and which class is in any case too numerous, and unable to obtain a decent standard of living as a consequence.

'Such people are a ready field in which to sow the seeds of every form of discontent, for they have just sufficient education to be a great trouble to the less scholastically educated but more stable mass of the population, as well as to properly constituted authority.

'Such an education *for the mass* acts like a corrosive in the community, undermining the solidarity of the tribal peoples.'

Dress and the Inferiority Complex

I have already discussed at length the whole philosophy of

dress and have hinted that the sharp contrast between the normal tribal dress and our own is one cause of the inferiority complex that threatens the people of NEFA. For while on one side this complex is fostered by deep social and cultural conflicts, on another it depends to no small degree on externals.

Subconsciously at least, the effect on the tribal mind of a large body of officials attired in a different dress helps to create the feeling that whatever is tribal is somehow inferior. If, therefore, our officers — and their wives — adopt certain elements of tribal dress, they not only fit better into the landscape and come nearer to their people, but they help to counteract this unhappy type of mental depression.

We are not to be fanatical about this — no one, for example, would suggest that the Political Officer of Subansiri should go about in an Apa Tani tail. And we recognise that it is much easier to use tribal dress in some areas than in others. There is no hardship in Kameng for an officer to wear the warm, appropriate and aesthetically pleasing Monpa dress: it would be less easy for him to adopt the Konyak ornaments! And in the foothills of Tirap, for example, the Noctes (who have been detribalized by generations of contact with the plains) regard an officer who puts on the local dress with suspicion. But the great majority of the people appreciate it and it undoubtedly does much good.

Some of our senior officers have already set an example in this. For example, the P.O. of Tuensang has had a special hat made for ceremonial occasions. An A.P.O. in Siang regularly wears an Adi hat instead of a topi. Officers in Lohit use fine Mishmi coats as dinner-jackets. The P.O. of Siang and members of his staff compete with one another in the colours and designs of their Adi coats. The P.O. of Kameng regularly wears Monpa dress. The Commandant and officers of the 2nd Battalion, Assam Rifles, wear Mishmi coats in the mess with their evening dress and the coats go very well with white shirts and black ties. When Shri N. K. Rustomji, former Adviser, visited Delhi and Shillong recently, he wore on all occasions a complete Sikkimese outfit and looked very well in it. Some of the senior officers' wives too use the local skirts and shawls, nor need they be ashamed to do so, for a good Mishmi or Naga shawl will add beauty to the most beautiful of wives.

The dress of tribal employees presents a special problem. Some of these are proud of their own attire, and come to greet you in splendid ceremonial hats and colourful ornaments which go well with their red coats. But others adopt European fashions because these are supposed to give additional importance and prestige. In India the sola topi is no longer worn by Europeans, to whom it has become the subject of rather corny jokes; but the minor official, the Sub-Inspector of Police, the Forest Ranger has adopted it as a sign of power. In the same way, a tribal chaprassi in NEFA who has a topi or a homburg hat, a pair of boots, perhaps even a pair of spectacles is in a better position to throw his weight about than if he was in his own traditional dress. This helps to create a sense of inferiority among the mass of the people.

Many years ago Dr Hutton made a suggestion to the Baptist Mission which was ignored, but which I revive here, for applied to our own Administration there is much in it of value.

'It is difficult to see why the taste for colour and brilliant effects which the Naga posesses should not be turned to the glory of God instead of being regarded as an offence before him. If the bright cloths, worn as a reward for the giving of Feasts of Merit by the ancients, were retained by the Christians for their own acts of social service; if the insignia of renown in war were made badges of rank in the congregation, and deacons and pastors encouraged to wear hornbill feathers and cowrie aprons to denote their office, while those assembling for divine worship were encouraged to do honour to the occasion by dressing in their best; if they were encouraged to adorn their church buildings with carvings, as they have done their morungs and their log-drums in the past, it is hard for a layman to see how the Deity would be dishonoured thereby, while their unquestionable artistic sense would be encouraged and possibly imbued with fresh vigour.'

Culture-change hits everyone at different angle — and in the case of our own employees its main target is the hat. We have suggested that we might have for each division the most honourable kind of local head-gear, with badges representing the Ashoka pillar attached in front, to present to those employees who have done good work and proved their loyalty.

In Kameng, for example, we might have the very fine Kalimpong hats which have a crown of yellow silk rising above a brim of fur. In Siang there are cane hats decorated with red and black hair. Some of the hats of the Subansiri Chiefs are most imposing. In the Tirap and Tuensang Divisions there are several varieties of Naga hats; many of these used to be adorned with head-hunting trophies; they may now be distinguished by the pillar of peace.

It is important that all this sort of thing should be done tactfully and without compulsion. A former Deputy-Commissioner of the Naga Hills fined anyone who came into his presence in western clothes, refused scholarships to any boy in shorts and shirt, denied promotion or even employment to any Naga who did not wear his national dress. We do not want to do that kind of thing. We should not force even tribal things on the tribal people if they do not want it.

Allies, not rivals

It is obvious that a valuable cure for the inferiority complex will be to recognise and use wherever possible the existing tribal institutions, and indeed we are already utilizing the village and tribal councils for planning development schemes and for the settlement of disputes, and we normally operate through the traditional authority of the local Chiefs and headmen.

Some of our junior officers have shown considerable imagination in this. For example, a young Block Development Officer in Namsang, faced with a problem of persuading the Noctes to take up the building of a road on a self-help basis, gathered the members of the tribal council together in a morung and sat with them, not as a superior official but as a fellow-Indian equally concerned with village affairs. The council debated the matter from eight in the evening till four o'clock the following morning and as each of the different Chiefs declared his willingness to take up half a mile or so of road-making, the young men thundered on the great log-drum that stood there. The result was that by morning the people felt that the plan had not been imposed upon them but was their own plan and had been ratified by the beating of the sacred drum.

So too a Base Superintendent in the remote outpost of Wakka, faced with the need of providing acccmmodation for visiting Wanchos, did not put up one of the conventional rest-houses but built a morung in the local style complete with drum. When the foundations were laid, the tribal priests came and performed the necessary ceremonies. This was greatly appreciated by the local people.

The same principle, of working through the local institutions and not in rivalry to them, can be applied to our medical activities.

One of the major difficulties in the way of persuading tribal people in all parts of India to come for medical treatment is the fact that they themselves have a fully developed system of diagnosis and treatment. The usual theory of disease in tribal society is that it is caused by hostile spirits, the ghosts of the dead, or the breach of some taboo. What is spiritually caused, therefore, must be spiritually cured, and this is the main reason why the people prefer to go to their own doctors rather than to our's.

There is no doubt that the tribal theory of disease is a deterrent to many who would otherwise come to our dispensaries and hospitals for treatment, and it is natural that the doctors should, therefore, regard the tribal priest as a dangerous professional rival.

But I do not think this need be so. A pious invalid in Europe will send both for the priest and the physician. The priest will pray for him, the physician will give him a pill. The theory is that God answers the priest's prayer by making the pill more efficacious: the physician is the instrument through which the divine compassion works.

We have suggested a similar compromise to the doctors in NEFA. The doctor and the medicine-man should learn to be allies and not rivals. The doctors must cease to be antagonistic to the system of tribal diagnosis and cure, cease to sneer at it as 'superstitious' and extend to it the sympathy they would feel for any other kind of faith-healing, of which there are ample examples in all the great world-religions.

A wise doctor in NEFA will make friends with the local priests, invite them to visit his hospital and let them offer prayers and make sacrifices for his patients, explaining that his own way of treatment is supplementary to their's. For the old methods are not without their value. Many diseases are at least partly due to mental causes — anxiety (peptic ulcers), guilt or fear (indigestion), frustration (constipation). Where a patient believes that his illness is due to sin or breach of some taboo, the priest can, by offering the appropriate sacrifices, remove the sense of guilt and attendant anxiety which is itself a potent cause of ill-health. If the patient thinks he is ill because a ghost or demon has attacked him, the priest can remove the fear and restore confidence by appeasing the offended spirit. His work thus has a really valuable psychological function, for it can promote the will-to-live, which is one of the most important needs in a case of tribal sickness.

Whenever a hospital or dispensary is opened or when the foundations of such buildings are laid (tribal people attach great importance to the foundations and sacrifices are generally offered at this time), the local priests should be invited to perform rites of blessing and protection. If the elaborate bamboo altars which are erected in Siang, Lohit and Subansiri were to stand before our medical buildings, the people would feel more at home and would come more readily. Our hospitals must grow out of the landscape if they are to succeed.

The essential thing is for our medical staff to take the right attitude to tribal medicine and the tribal priest. The most successful of our doctors have been those who have interested themselves in what we may call medical sociology, in such things as the tribal pharmacopoeia, the tribal theory of the influence of dreams on health, tribal methods of diagnosis. The subject is fascinating in itself, and to study it almost automatically changes a man's attitude and thus helps to win the confidence of the local people.

We should never make fun of the tribal priests and doctors in our Variety Shows or on other occasions. Elsewhere in tribal India, officials have attempted to wean the people away from their own traditions by mockery, by criticism, even by abuse. This does not succeed; it only makes the tribesmen feel alien from us and creates in them a sense of inferiority and resentment.

The people do not yet feel that the hospitals and dispensaries are *their's*. They belong to the Government and the patients who go to them are introduced into a strange, alarming, almost wholly alien world. We are now trying to make things more familiar, give patients their own clothes and blankets, have health-charts with their own tribal background, hang the walls of a ward with good photographs of local tribal scenes, talk to them in their own language, permit the consolations of the tribal priests. This will have an appreciable influence towards acclimatizing modern medicine in NEFA.

The Danger of Pauperization

The custom of trying to keep the tribesmen happy and content by giving them presents is very old, and the obligations of century-old *posa* gifts are still with us. In the British period, officers on tour gave extravagant presents, not all of the most appropriate kind: in Lohit, for example, opium was distributed as a 'political present'; in Subansiri ugly and unsuitable gifts of cloth impaired the natural taste of the people; and everywhere rum was one of the most popular ways of establishing friendly relations.

The custom has continued to the present time, but in a modified form and, of course, the giving of opium and rum has now been stopped. Three years ago the Political Officers' Conference passed a resolution urging the reduction of political presents in the settled areas to a minimum, and more recently a comprehensive directive has been issued ordering the gradual reduction of presents and prescribing the kind of things to be given.

On a tour of exploration a suitable gift may make the difference between hostility and friendliness; in the more settled villages, the Chiefs are often obliging and hospitable and suffer without complaint the dislocation of their daily work that is inevitably caused by an official visit. To give a few leaders a present as a reward for services rendered is a graceful and pleasant act. In this case the word 'present' is incorrect; it is a courteous way of making payment for services rendered.

But there are certain dangers in this practice. In some places presents are expected as a right and there have been cases in the past when Chiefs have returned a gift as insufficiently expensive. I have found too, especially among the Konyaks and the tribes of northern Subansiri, a distressing habit of begging, begging on a rather large and persistent scale. An officer's camp, or a Divisional Headquarters, should not be regarded as a sort of store where you can get free goods.

A great deal depends on the kind of things we give. If they are chosen with intelligence, they may help to promote tribal art and industries. When Shri Jairamdas Daulatram visited Tuensang in 1955, he distributed as many as four hundred bundles of yarn there and two hundred more at Mon. He ordered two hundred pieces of steel for daos. He gave away two-and-a-half maunds of cowrie shells for ornamental dresses and a large quantity of beads. If our officers would follow this admirable example much harm would be avoided.

The Administration has now ordered that yarn, beads, cowrie shells, agricultural implements, soap, salt and tea should be the commonest presents given and that where cloth has to be given it should be locally woven. Where cloth of any kind is given it should not normally be white, but of some gay colour.

Although some parts of NEFA are very 'colourful', there are great tracts of drabness, where colour is a psychological as well as an artistic need, a need which can be met by gifts of yarn and the development of the dyeing industry. The application of aesthetics to benevolence will help to meet this need.

But in any case yarn is a far better gift than cloth. Gifts of cloth have had a bad effect on the psychology of the people; they have debased their taste; they have discouraged the hand-loom industry; and in some cases they have been abused by officers who have traded them for food-supplies.

Even where the people have little to wear (though actually there are few such places), and a humanitarian instinct urges us to make presents of cloth, it would be better to introduce yarn and weaving so that they can make their own clothes, rather than to give unsuitable clothes which may permanently injure their good taste and their self-reliance.

Allied to the problem of political presents is the question of relief. This needs to be considered against the background of the traditional self-reliance and co-operation of the tribes. I have seen how, when a house is burnt down, the people from half-a-dozen neighbouring villages assemble with wood, bamboo and thatch and help to rebuild it. I have often seen a village co-operating to repair a house for some poor widow. In the old days the tribesmen themselves built bridges and made paths.

There was formerly a danger that an over-generous policy of giving relief at almost every emergency would destroy this fine spirit among the people. Obviously, one's first instinct is to pour out assistance to the poor wherever they are in need, but we do need to ask ourselves whether the ultimate result will be good. In Madhya Pradesh the tribal people today only reluctantly take up any corporate activity, such as cleaning a well or mending a tank; everything is the business of the Government. I have found this attitude in parts of NEFA; it is not 'our business' to clear a path or mend a bridge—Government must do it. And it may well come about that if someone's house is burnt down, the fine spirit of tribal relief will no longer operate and the people will say, 'Let Government see to it'.

To save the people from pauperization, to preserve the spirit of self-help and self-reliance, to maintain the ideal of co-operation and neighbourliness, the Administration has decided that relief should be given only in exceptional and tragic cases. Here again, the kind of relief to be given is most important. The provision of food, and still more seed, does not pauperize the people when it is given in a real emergency. But the distribution of cloth, utensils, blankets, and other things may have a thoroughly bad psychological effect, especially when the things distributed are not natural to the tribal scene. Blouses, towels, singlets, and all sorts of foreign utensils have been given in the past to people who had never used them. It may be that the blouse and the singlet will come—but it need not come as a result of having one's house burn down. Moreover, this constant distribution of foreign things is in itself a way of imposing our ways and manners on the people, and is thus contrary to our fundamental policy.

A special type of pauperization, which has a singularly bad subconscious effect in impressing on the people a sense of having a lower status, is the custom of officers and their wives giving away their cast-off clothes. Some of the tribal people themselves are bad about this; they come begging for an old shirt, a pair of trousers, a blouse; if one of them is employed as a house-servant, it is so easy to dress him up in one of master's shirts.

But this amiable habit should be resisted. The people of NEFA are not paupers to be turned into clowns with second-hand clothing; they are traditionally a proud people, and though a former thoughtless and undirected tradition has done something to make them servile, we must at all costs now bring it to an end. This applies equally to the Assam Rifles and Army Engineers, some of whom are sincerely generous, as well as to the civil staff. Generosity can often do more harm than good.

Once when I was in Margherita, a Nocte girl came to the Political Officer's office (which at that time was in the town) complaining that her money had been stolen. Asked what she had been intending to spend it on, she replied that she had come down from her village to buy some cloth. Kindly subordinates immediately suggested that, as she had been robbed by civilization, civilization should repay the debt, and that she should be given cloth or money equivalent to what she had lost. The Political Officer, however, had a better idea: he asked her if she could weave. She said that she could and he therefore presented her with a bundle of yarn (of colours suitable to her tribe) and suggested that she should herself weave the cloth she needed. She was delighted and went away consoled.

This little incident is to my mind a parable of the proper way of bringing relief to those in need.

Unintelligent benevolence can be as great a menace to the tribesman's character as intelligent exploitation can be to his pocket.

Architecture

Throughout NEFA, and specially in Siang, Subansiri and Lohit, there is great scope for improvement of the tribal house. The Adis, Daflas and others have a curious incapacity to make a floor; in many places the walls too are badly constructed and afford little protection against the cold wind and the rain. The style of the houses need not be changed but the technique of the building could be improved. We can best effect this improvement by example, but if the architectural style of our official buildings continues to be alien to the local style, it is not likely to have much influence. On the other hand, if some of the buildings follow the local tribal design, but improve on it in technique, then the tribesmen would copy it to their advantage.

In Tuensang and Tirap the schools might well be made in the morung style; in Siang an improved dormitory would be natural and appropriate; in Kameng there is no reason why we should not follow the local architecture — in western Kameng indeed the houses of the villagers are considerably better than those of most of the officers and the schools.

I have frequently been painfully impressed by the cheerlessness of our schools. I have been told by teachers that boys do not attend because they are so cold. When asked why they do not have a fire, they point out that the style of the building is such that you cannot have a fire in it.

Tribal people do everything in circles; the schools are made in straight lines and rectangles. In other words, tribals like to sit round a fire, to gather in a circle round a teacher or lecturer. Our benches in tidy rows, our dreary rooms with never a fire in them, the regimentation in lines and rectangles is unfamiliar. Why could we not have fires and logs of wood, or at least low desks in the traditional Indian style, round them, so that the boys could sit at these instead of on benches and silly little desks? Boarders too sleep in cold rooms without fires — no tribal ever does that at home; he always sleeps by a fire.

Although it would be, as I have suggested earlier, desirable that all our buildings should grow out of the landscape and should fit completely into the picture, experience has shown that this may not be possible in the Headquarter townships and in some of the outposts. After all, a house evolves itself according to the use to which it is to be put and the house of a Political Officer is thus bound to be different from that of a tribal Chief. On the other hand, many of the official buildings, such as schools, hostels, CITPC institutions, ASC barracks, H.D. Homes and homes for the destitute, rest-houses both for the staff and for the tribal people in the interior should certainly be in the local style of architecture with a number of obvious improvements.

Architecture varies greatly from Division to Division and in most places the style of a building is as much a criterion of a certain tribe as its style of hair-dressing. For example, if you ask a Minyong how he differs from a Gallong, he will reply that both his men and women cut their hair short while the Gallongs allow it to grow long, and that he builds his house as a long rectangle whereas a Gallong makes it square. There is all the diffeernce in the world between a house in Tuensang and a Mishmi house in Lohit or again a Monpa house in western Kameng. It is impossible, therefore, for us to lay down any general rule whereby the architecture and general design of tribal houses should be improved and in actual fact, it would be an impertinence for us to attempt to do so. These houses have gradually evolved throughout the centuries to meet certain necessities of the climate and the conditions of daily life. For example, while a good many of the houses have fairly high roofs and some of them (such as the homes of the Konyak or Wancho Chiefs) have very high roofs indeed, others have rather low ceilings. It is probable that the reason for this is danger from the storms that sweep across the country and often blow down our own official buildings.

But there are, as I have already hinted, certain aspects of the tribal architecture which can everywhere be developed. First and foremost is the floor. If we could teach the people to make good plank floors, it would add greatly to the warmth of the house, for at present the wind whistles up through the broken and badly constructed bamboo floors; it would prevent unhealthy smells and insects coming up from below, and it would make it much more easy to keep the house clean. It is difficult to use a broom on a bamboo floor, but a wooden floor can easily be swept.

Then again one of the greatest drawbacks of a tribal house is the smoke. The burning of wood fires, often fed with green branches, fills the houses, which have no kind of chimney, with thick clouds of smoke and these inflame the eyes and cover everything with a layer of dust. We have already devised a sort of chimney which can be introduced above the hearth without disturbing the main design of the building and if that can be widely used, it will mean a great improvement in the health of the people, particularly in the condition of their eyes.

Other forms of ventilation will prove more difficult. Some tribes make windows in their houses and I have stayed in Mishmi, Monpa, Wancho and Adi houses which have been well lighted and ventilated. Other houses are dark and stuffy. We must remember, however, that here too the architecture has evolved to meet certain needs and the lack of windows is sometimes intended to keep out stinging insects, protect from cold and ensure, in the congested conditions of village life, some sort of privacy.

For official buildings which are made mainly for tribal occupation, I feel that we should always have the following features:—

(1) Every house should be raised well off the ground. Except in the case of some of the great Konyak houses, almost everywhere

in NEFA buildings are raised on piles. Nobody would ever dream of living on the damp and dirty ground.

(2) Every house should have a sitting-platform either at the end or along the side. This is an important element in NEFA village life, for the people love to sit out in the sun whenever possible and in, for example, a CITCP Hostel for girls, the trainees should certainly be encouraged to do their weaving on the platform out of doors when it is fine.

(3) The indoor life of the people centres round the fire. Some tribes regard the hearth as of such great importance that they give special names to each of its sides and there are rules as to who may sit at each, and the kind of work which may be done there. It is perfectly easy to introduce a hearth even into a floor that is well raised above the ground, and the tribal people themselves have already solved the difficulty; we might well imitate them.

We are also trying, wherever possible, to copy and develop the local models for such buildings as schools, barracks, hostels and H.D. Sanatoria. In Tawang, for example, the local staff told me that they had no doubt that many more patients would come if we could rebuild the existing Home as a Monpa village. The present Leprosy Home, which was erected a number of years ago, is very much of an 'institution'. There are wards in which two or perhaps three patients have to live together, a thing which Monpas especially dislike. These wards have no hearths and the kitchens are in separate buildings fifty to a hundred yards away. I was told that it was very difficult to persuade the patients to sit in their clean but cold and cheerless rooms and that instead they preferred, and naturally, to spend all day in the kitchen by the fire. If we can build double-storeyed stone houses on the Monpa pattern, with sitting-platforms, and hearths in the middle of the living-rooms, I have no doubt that many more people will come for treatment. We will have a Gompa in the home for their consolation, and among the traditional Buddhist paintings on the walls there may well be one of Gandhiji tending the lepers at Sevagram. We are in fact building the Leprosy Homes at Along and Pasighat according to the local Adi style with a number of special improvements. The general design of the buildings will be the same. The lay-out of the Home will be like that of an actual village but we will give planks for walls and floors and use CIG sheets (which I hope will be painted a good colour) for the roofs.

In these and other ways, we will be able to make our buildings more homely and natural. There is great psychological value in making people feel at home.

There is, however, a difficulty in the rules governing all engineering enterprizes. The regulations about plinth-areas, payment at so much a square foot and so on are a serious obstacle to implementing our policy, and if we are not to impose stereotyped and unsuitable buildings on NEFA, it is essential that the rules should be liberalized.

'Through their own Team'

The ultimate solution of the inferiority complex is to train up the people of NEFA to do the work which at present we are presuming to do for them. Once they realise that the future is their's, they will be able to keep their heads high. On this the Prime Minister has spoken at length as follows:

'It is obvious that these areas have to progress. But it is equally obvious that they have to progress in their own way. They have their own likes. They do not like something alien to be imposed upon them. No individual can grow in alien surroundings, habits, or customs. How are we going to keep these two things together? It is not an easy problem... We have to find a middle course. And that can only succeed if the people are in harmony with it and co-operate with it and there is no element of compulsion about it. That approach also has ultimately to be applied through their own people.

'The first thing, therefore, is to train their own people who can work among them and that will be far more effective than for outsiders to try... We have to make them progress, but progress does not mean just an attempt to duplicate what we have got in any part of India. It may not be suitable to them. It may not be suitable even to India. But there are many things in India which are suitable to them. They will adopt them gradually. Any element of imposition has to be absent so far as possible and so people have to be trained to train others. It may not be a very rapid progress. Every kind of training takes time. Whatever profession you may adopt, it takes years to train people, engineers, doctors and so on. It is better to go ahead on a firm basis than merely to knock about with odd jobs here and there. There is a tendency to do odd jobs in improving them without any firm outlook'.

The cardinal principle of the Second Five Year Plan, as the Adviser, Shri K. L. Mehta, has remarked recently, 'is to provide special facilities for the training of the inhabitants of NEFA themselves. The intention is that the increasing demand for personnel as a result of the implementation of our schemes should be met from among the local people to the maximum extent possible. Our key institutions such as the Extension Training Centre, the Basic Education Training Centre, and the Health Training Centre will have to shoulder a very large responsibility in meeting this challenge. To mention only a few, we have to train school-teachers, compounders and agricultural staff in the shortest possible time. We hope that it will not be long before doctors, engineers and indeed administrators can be found from among the residents of NEFA. This, to my mind, is the crux of the problem.'

But even now, before this plan can be fully implemented, we are already trying to associate the tribal people in every possible way with the work of the Administration. As Shri K. L. Mehta has said again: 'The inculcation of self-confidence in the people is perhaps the most important single factor in bringing success in the type of work we are attempting to do. We must give them opportunities to participate even at the elementary stage of working out schemes for their own betterment. The success of our policy will depend on our ability to blend the demands of modern technology and the subjective demands of the people with the moral demand, which has been explained as "the universal right of man to make significant choices".

'I doubt whether we are still doing as much as we should to develop a sense of confidence and pride amongst the people and at the same time to give them scope to solve their own problems. In other words we should act in accordance with a recent Community Project slogan that all development programmes should be regarded by the people as *their* programmes and that Government steps in only to help them in fulfilling them speedily and efficiently, in our case along the lines of their own genius.' Development is for the people, not the people for development.

Part Five

RELIGIOUS AIMS IN NEFA

The problem of religion in NEFA is a complex one, for the sudden impact and rapid development to which the people have been exposed is without precedent, and it is thus not easy to predict what their reactions will be. In other parts of tribal India, where the process of acculturation has been spread over a hundred years, the tribesmen have gradually assimilated elements of Hinduism such as the adoption of social and food taboos, a change in the names of the old gods to relate them to the deities of the Hindu pantheon, and a more elevated notion of the Supreme Being. A certain number, but few compared to the large numbers converted in Assam, have adopted an entirely new religion such as Christianity or Islam.

What then is likely to happen in NEFA? In ten years time there will be a considerable body of educated young men and women. Will they find it possible to maintain their faith in the old religions? Will they return to their villages and introduce religious reforms as many educated Hindus reformed Hinduism in the last century? Or will they adopt a new religion, Buddhism, Hinduism or Christianity?

I doubt if the NEFA tribals will accept Hinduism in any organized manner. Between them and that great religion stands the gentle figure of the cow. Yet there are many things which should attract them in popular Hinduism: the same belief in a supreme deity ruling over a host of lesser spirits; the same sacrifices; the same colourful festivals; myths and legends of a rather similar pattern. But the tribal people, even the educated ones, will not give up their mithun, beef and alcohol; they are likely to reject the caste system, the new and unfamiliar taboos, the prevailing Puritanism.

Christianity has made an appeal to the tribals of Assam (though, curiously enough, it has had very little success in Middle India and Orissa) because it has been associated in their minds with the idea of progress. Christianity in the past has meant hospitals, education, the English language, a larger richer material life, a gospel of universal brotherhood. Its flexibility with regard to food rules has more than compensated for its rigidity about such matters as rice-beer and polygamy.

A number of people, themselves Christians by faith, believe that the best solution of the religious question in NEFA is to admit Indian missionaries and to encourage a general Christianization of the tribes. If the form of Christianity introduced was of a liberal kind and truly national in spirit, this would, they argue, bring many spiritual benefits to the people, and would save the educated from adopting an irreligious and materialist outlook. Since many tribals in the Autonomous Districts are already Christian, the people of NEFA could then be united with them in one Frontier State, in which there would be a natural religious unity and no place for communal dissension. In any case, the people will not retain their old religion.

I do not see why this should be so. Indeed the very assumption suggests that, however much we may protest to the contrary and even accept consciously, there is a deep-rooted belief in the subconscious that whatever is tribal is somehow inferior.

But a careful study of tribal religion, both in NEFA and elsewhere, does not suggest that it is noticeably inferior to its competitors. It has its drawbacks, it is undeveloped, there are many problems to which it has no answer. But as a working way of life it brings consolation to its adherents and gives them hope and courage.

The religious systems of NEFA have five qualities which, in so far as it is possible to measure these things at all, are of fundamental value.

1. There is a very general belief in a Supreme God who is just, benevolent and good. For example, Doini-Pollo, the Sun-Moon god of all the Adi groups, is regarded as the great witness in the sky, the upholder of truth. Let us go to one of the most primitive of the tribes for an opinion. In the Sipi Valley I noted down the terms of an invocation which a Tagin priest addressed to Doini-Pollo in the course of a test to determine whether someone was a thief or not:

> 'You are the greatest of all; you are above all; you see all. You see the lost things, the stolen things. At night, you watch the world of the dead. In the day, from the world below,

having feasted well, you come in your finest clothes, with splendid ornaments, a shining dao in your hand. You look on every side; you know everything'.

Although this august being does not seem to have created the world, he reigns unchallenged in the heavens; he is 'the eye of the world'; he is as important to man as the eye is to the body. He watches everything; he is the witness of truth; he shows men the way to go; he protects them; he treats them with mercy. Above all, he is the lord of truth and an oath taken on his name is the most binding of all. Though he is not offered special sacrifices, for he does not need them, his name is invoked on every ritual occasion. He is the unifying force behind popular religion from the Siang to the Upper Kamla and perhaps beyond, and it may well be that he will provide a basis whereby Adi religion can develop along the lines of the Truth and Goodness which are his most conspicuous attributes. After all, the Sun is a very ancient god and has been worshipped by comparatively sophisticated civilizations.

Similar notions are held by other tribal groups, though sometimes we find, as in Wancho and Konyak thought, that the benevolent Sky-god is opposed by a malevolent Earth-god; earthquakes are caused by the titanic wars between them.

One more example may be given. Chungba-Sangyat seems to be a pre-Buddhist deity who is still worshipped by the Sherdukpens who have developed an interesting synthesis of Buddhist and tribal ideas. Chungba-Sangyat's chief quality is his mercy and pity for mankind. He delivers a young hero who calls on him in his despair. He saves a magic deer threatened with poison and removes the evil from its body. Although he is neither omniscient nor omnipotent, he is great, powerful and benevolent.

Surely there is no reason why an educated tribesman should be ashamed of ideas such as these.

It is true that beneath these mighty rulers of the unseen world, there is a host of demons and furies who prey upon mankind. But similar conceptions are to be found in popular Hinduism today and for centuries the sable wings of Satan overshadowed the sunlit teachings of Jesus Christ.

2. In the second place there is in tribal religion a genuine emphasis on the spiritual realities behind the life of everyday.

The belief in a circumambient unseen world, in which gods and men, the quick and the dead, are one great family; the faith in kindly tutelary spirits, to whom priests are 'married'; the emphasis on the spiritual cause of tragedy — these things do at least point the way from a merely material and temporal estimate of life, and lay the foundations for a development of higher values.

3. Then tribal religion is built up from an elaborate mythology. A recent American writer has pointed out that myth, at its best, 'is to be regarded as a recognition of the drama of human existence. Its ultimate aim is not the wishful distortion of the world, but rather serious comprehension and envisagement of its fundamental nature. Myth is regarded as representing metaphorically a world-picture and insight into life generally and may, therefore, be considered as primitive philosophy or metaphysical thought.' If this is true, as I think it is, it means that the NEFA tribes have their own philosophy of religion, even though it is expressed in poetic or metaphorical form. In the tribal Puranas, as we may call them, we find a strong sense of history, a pride in the descent of the race from a great ancestor, the record of heroic deeds and, most interestingly, traces of a belief in the value of supreme self-sacrifice for the good of mankind. A noble king dies out of pity for the sufferings of men and thus brings the boon of death to the world. A great personage, on whose belly men once lived, dies for fear that he may injure his tenants. A tree falls and dies so that by its death the earth and sky may be perfected. The idea is crudely expressed; yet this deep and notable ideal is there: that one may die that all may live.

4. Tribal religion is associated with a social ethic that unites the tribe in its discipline and undoubtedly makes for a certain nobility of conduct. The great tribal virtues are discipline, devotion to work, generosity and hospitality, truth, kindness. Many tribes, while permitting considerable freedom to the unmarried, insist on a high standard of marital fidelity. The folk-tales of the tribes that have come under Buddhist influence stress the gentle virtues of mercy and compassion.

This ethic is not related to the religion in the sense that virtue will normally be rewarded and vice punished in the after-life. But the absence of an eschatology of rewards and punishments is no disadvantage: it rather links tribal religion with the most advanced ethical and religious systems.

5. Finally, tribal religion gives the people the power to reconcile themselves to the eternal emergencies of life. It has been said that fear is the father of religion and love its late-born daughter, and it is true that there is an element of fear in all primitive religion. But this is true also of the great world religions, and a celebrated psychologist has pointed out that a merely 'healthy-minded' and optimistic religion may prove inadequate when faced with the deeper tragedies of existence.

In their religion, the tribesmen have created a realistic picture of life seen *sub specie eternitatis;* they face it, in all its dismal trappings, with courage; yet it is not fear of things as they are, but a heroic appreciation of them which has brought it into being. The tribesmen are realists; till recently they lived a life of constant anxiety and they projected this onto the wider canvas of their theology. Today, as they discover a more friendly world on earth, they may come to believe in a kinder world in heaven.

Above all, the tribesmen have faced the problem of death; they have not solved it any more than we have solved it; but they have devised means whereby it can be made more tolerable. The lengthy course of funerary ceremonial, the elaborate tombs, the carvings, the feasts of mourning are not due only to a desire to propitiate the ghost; they give the mourners an opportunity of separating themselves psychologically from the departed object, always a protracted and painful process. Modern psychology suggests that their efforts are well adapted to this end.

The tribesmen believe in a life after death and that living and dead continue to be united in one family.

Such are the advantages of tribal religion. On the other hand, it may be argued that this type of faith has given sanction to practices that are now universally condemned, such as head-hunting and human sacrifice. This, of course, is true and it must be admitted that the suppression of these practices has left a serious cultural and religious gap in the life of the Naga groups.

It is hard for anyone to approach this subject with complete objectivity. The Hindu, despite himself, considers whether the tribal religions cannot in some way be brought within the all-embracing tolerance of Hinduism; the Christian cannot help regarding them as rivals tc his own universal faith; the agnostic looks on all religions, tribal as well as others, as bound to collapse before the spread of scientific knowledge.

In their pictures of the future, Huxley, Forster and Orwell (to name no others) give us a world in which religion, at least as we understand it, has no place; C. S. Lewis, on the other hand, believes that the Christian religion will in the end triumph over science and pictures a female Pope reigning on the planet Mars. At present, whatever the rationalists may say, there is every sign that science is not in fact destroying religious faith. The extraordinary success of Buchmanism and Billy Graham in the scientific west and the swing towards religion in the ancient universities of Oxford and Cambridge suggests that the human mind is incurably religious.

Tribal religion, developed and reformed from within, is thus not bound to be destroyed by science.

In one of his rare utterances on tribal problems, Mahatma Gandhi urged that the tribesmen should be persuaded to abolish animal sacrifice and the use of alcohol in worship. It is probably true that these are the main features which divide the tribal from other religions in India. Yet, although there is much to be done in the way of teaching the tribesmen to kill their animals before the altar more mercifully, the general practice of animal sacrifice is more innocuous than it sounds. In 'civilized' life, one's meat is provided by the butcher; in tribal life, it is provided by the clergyman. The sacrifice is a sacrament, where the people eat in the name of the gods. To give the sanction of religion to the eating of meat may offend the vegetarian, but it surely cannot be regarded as offensive to the religious spirit.

I submit, therefore, that we should not be defeatist about tribal religion. It is worthy of preservation; I believe that it contains the seeds of growth. Anyone who reads Sir James Frazer's *Folk-lore of the Old Testament* may see from what humble beginnings two of the great world-religions have developed.

The essential point in this new attitude is that we should no longer assume that as the tribal people become educated and enter into contact with the outside world, they are necessarily bound to abandon their traditional faith. It has previously been supposed that an educated tribal is almost inevitably bound to become a Hindu or a Christian. Today we feel that, while he is of course at perfect liberty to change his religion if he so desires, it need not be necessary for him to do so. The deeper study of the tribal religions outlined in the previous pages shows that they have many elements that satisfy the heart, even though, like other religions, they have other elements which do not satisfy the mind. We should be able to provide a climate in which the old religions can grow and reform themselves *from within* so that ultimately there will be in NEFA religious concepts that will be truly in character, yet having a wider view and a purer conception of God and man.

If we are to achieve this, there are certain things that we ourselves should do:

(*i*) The first is that we should study and try to understand the religion of the areas where we live. This is not only a fascinating pastime but, if it is done with tact and sincerity, will in itself help to encourage the tribal people in their faith.

(*ii*) The second is to extend to tribal religion that attitude of sincere respect which we are trying to give to tribal life and institutions generally. No one should on any account criticise or laugh at any tribal ceremony or belief. Sometimes the work of a well-trained higher officer may be completely undone by the ignorant folly of a clerk or a jawan. The same reverence should be shown by all members of the staff, should they be present at any tribal ceremony, that they would show in a Christian church or Hindu temple.

(*iii*) We should be careful how we talk and about the words we use. Let us banish such expressions as 'superstition', 'heathen', 'devil dance' in relation to religion, just as we are trying to avoid generally such words as 'backward', 'uplift' and other patronizing expressions. We should not speak of 'animism' but we should speak of the 'Konyak religion' or the 'Adi religion', which will suggest that the tribal faith has for its adherents just as much authority and dignity as the faith of the outside world. Care should be taken in filling up any form, in which a person's religion is to be stated, that a tribesman should not be described as 'Hindu', 'Buddhist', 'Christian', unless he has formally adopted one of these religions or unless (as is the case in parts of Kameng) one of the world religions, here Buddhism, has long since been accepted by the whole tribe.

(*iv*) Similarly, officers should use the local word for the Supreme Being whenever they have to speak of God; and oaths should be taken on the same name. Some simple prayers addressed in the local name of God might be composed, and in time our Research Department will, we hope, give us collections of myths and legends and an account of the chief religions, which can be translated and which will help to create that feeling of dignity and confidence in one's own culture, which is a secret of tribal vitality. The mythological treasury of the NEFA tribes might well come to have for their modern educated youth the same sort of authority and provide the same kind of inspiration that the Book of Genesis and the great Hindu epics have for modern Christians and Hindus. We do not take the myths literally, but we recognise their symbolical importance and they supply some deep need of the human heart.

This matter is summed up in some wise words of Shri Jairamdas Daulatram:

'Just as Hindu society in Assam recoiled against the approach of the Christian proselytizing programme, so also will one day the tribal people recoil against our approach to them, if we fail to understand their life and culture in their true light and miss the spirit of their belief simply because its forms and terms seem to be different from what we are familiar with. We must shed our subtle sense of superiority which makes us picture ourselves as "reformers", commissioned to work for the uplift of the backward tribes... The people of the hills to the north and the south of the Brahmaputra are no more animists than the Hindus of the Assam Valley'.

This is the fundamental need — to create the right mental climate in which alone the tribal faiths can flourish. No one will take the trouble to be a reformer of something he has learnt to despise. As Shri Jairamdas says again, 'It needs a sympathetic atmosphere to mature and develop this germinal idea into a powerful source of spiritual inspiration which can model tribal life on an even higher level.'

Some such attitude as this is the basis of the Administration's attitude to missionaries of all religions. The Administration has been accused of being anti-Christian because it refuses to allow the Baptist missionaries to pass the Inner Line and has put certain restrictions on the building of churches and promotion of proselytizing. Nothing could be further from the truth. The NEFA Administration observes a policy of strict religious neutrality and would not even impose tribal religion on those who do not want it. The Administration takes exactly the same attitude to Hindu or Buddhist or Muslim missionaries as it does to Christian missionaries.

This is illustrated in the case of the songs and hymns sung in the schools, which we have insisted should be of a neutral character. The Prime Minister has noted that even the well-known hymn 'Raghupati Raghava Raja Ram' was 'totally inappropriate for the NEFA schools and this, along with others far more inappropriate, is no longer taught.

The reasons for not permitting missionaries is in the first place a political one. Unhappily the impact of the mission most concerned and its pastors has in actual practice been to create an anti-Indian sentiment, a fact for which there is overwhelming evidence. Even where the missionaries and pastors have not themselves engaged in any political activity, the psychological effect of their teaching, that only the Christians are saved and that the heathen (among whom must be counted the vast majority of the Indian people) will be damned, naturally introduces an element of division between the converts and the rest of India. Here theology, translated into politics, can have a dangerous effect.

Furthermore, proselytization divides village communities which we are only just beginning to unite. Hindu missionaries who teach teetotalism and vegetarianism, as well as a number of other taboos hitherto unknown to the tribal mind, are as divisive of the village unity and as destructive of tribal culture and custom as the Christian missionaries.

The cultural effect of missionary teaching has been fully described in a note in the Census of India 1931, an official document which may be quoted here. The reader should bear in mind that the British Government of the day had nc prejudice against missions as such: rather the opposite. It is the cultural, not the religious aspect which is being considered

'Realising that on the preservation of customs developed exactly to fit the environment and tested by centuries of use depends the whole fabric of tribal society, Government has been at pains to preserve them to the utmost limit possible and to ensure that such change as much inevitably come shall not be destructive in its suddenness.

'In strong contrast has been the attitude of the American Baptist Mission. As religion plays a part in every Naga ceremony and as that religion is not Christianity, every ceremony must go. Such ceremonies as the great Feasts of Merit, at which the whole village, rich and poor alike, is entertained, and of which the religious aspect is far less important than the social, have not been remodelled on Christian lines, but have been utterly abolished among converts. This has been the fate, too, of all village sacrificial feasts. The place of these is not adequately taken by small parties meeting to drink tea.

'The suppression among Baptists of the ancient feasts in which all joined is not only a loss to the would-be hosts, but to the village as a whole, and not least to the poor, who always get their full share of good cheer at such festivals. To abolish these feasts is to do away with the very few occassions on which the awful monotony of village life is broken. They are, too, the natural Naga and Kuki way of distributing wealth. I have heard a Baptist teacher boast that his granaries were so full of the store of years that some of the grain was black with age. Had he been a Naga that grain would not have been left to rot uselessly but would have been eaten by his fellow villagers.

'It is at the big feasts that singing and dancing are indulged in and full dress worn. These have been entirely suppressed among the Ao, Lhota and Sema Christians, the men of whom wear no ornaments at all, having stripped their beads from the necks, their ivory armlets from their arms and even the cotton wool from their ears. The women are more conservative and still often wear their beads, though I doubt if a girl would actually wear her ornaments at a Mission school. Angami men too are difficult to dislodge from their ancient ways. The best of them do not give up their picturesque dress and are quite ready to put on all their finery and take part in the ceremonial singing parties which are such a feature of their village life.

'Of the material arts in these hills wood-carving is the chief. It is displayed on the houses of those who have given the great Feasts of Merit, on the morung posts of the Aos, Konyaks and Lhotas, and on the big xylophones of the Aos. This is doomed to extinction as the power of the mission increases. Feasts of Merit are forbidden among them, and no attempt is made to induce rich Christians to decorate their houses in the old way. No Christian boy is allowed to go through his time in the morung and they are not built any more in Christian villages. In such villages, too the old xylophones can be seen rotting in the jungle.

'The suppression of the wearing of all ornaments or tribal finery, of dancing, of singing (except hymns), of village feasts and of all artistic outlet is spreading an unspeakable drabness over village life. Old songs and old traditions are being rapidly forgotten. Told year in and year out that all the past history, all the strivings, all the old customs of his tribe are wholly evil, the Naga tends to despise his own race, and no night of the soul is blacker than that.

'The suppression of the morung, in which young Nagas learn to be useful citizens, is unwarranted by any good reason that I have ever heard. It is part of the tendency to abolish old things just because they are old, and substitute for the strong communal feeling which has enabled the tribes to survive for so long an individualism which is really foreign to them. Not only is this individualism wrapped up with the strong emphasis on personal salvation; it is also the direct and natural reaction against the destruction of all the old things that mattered in village life and all the old expressions of the artistic and social genius of the tribe.'

We need not agree with every detail of this criticism, but we would do well to take warning from it. It is true that it deals mainly with the culturally destructive activities of a particular Mission. But we should remember that our own administrative and development activities, if wrongly directed, or Missions of other religions, can be just as inimical to the true spirit of tribal life.

Part Six

SOCIAL AIMS IN NEFA

'The tribes should develop their own culture and make their contribution to the cultural richness of the country. It is unnecessary to cause them to change their customs, habits or diversions so far as to make themselves indistinguishable from other classes. To do so would be to rob rural and pastoral life of its colour and stimulating diversity.'

— PANDIT G. B. PANT

It is not only presumptuous, but it may be positively dangerous. to interfere with the social life and organization of populations which differ greatly from ourselves, for not only may we make mistakes through ignorance, but we may — as the Prime Minister has warned us — in our eagerness to do good, do grievous harm instead.

In a recent UNESCO publication, *Interrelations of Cultures*, the distinguished French scholar, M. Griaulle, has stressed the dangers of interference with tribal culture and traditions:

'Whatever interferes with them is likely to harm the unconscious. To hustle them in order to get through stages of technical development more quickly and to make a clean sweep of institutions and beliefs on the ground that they impede progress, is to create repressions and traumatisms which may have catastrophic results for whole nations'.

I have already quoted the words of Gandhiji when some of his followers in South Africa complained to him about African nudity. 'When a large society follows a particular custom, it is quite possible that the custom is harmless enough even if it seems highly improper to the members of another society.'

But there are certain matters where Government has been compelled to intervene.

Law and Order

Perhaps the most important of these is in regard to law and

order. For centuries the people of NEFA have lived in a constant state of inter-tribal and inter-village war; they have had a long history of crisis and anxiety. Obviously this could not continue and Government has had to bring head-hunting to an end; it has had to stop the kidnapping of children as slaves, check the smuggling of opium, put a stop to cruel punishments, and prevent human sacrifice.

In 1931 Mr J. P. Mills wrote, in one of the Census of India Reports, an interesting note which presumably represented the official attitude of the day.

'Only two ancient customs have had to be put down by Government: the sacrifice of mithun by cruel methods, and head-hunting. The suppression of the first is wholly good, and more humane methods of killing can be substituted without detriment to the rites.

'The suppression of head-hunting, though necessary in any area which is fully administered, has probably not been for the benefit of the tribes. The very fact that, far from being an honour, it is a disgrace to be killed in war, makes all Nagas very careful of their own safety,and their wars were singularly innocuous affairs. In a war between two big villages each side might lose one or two men a year.

'The number of lives saved by the suppression of the practice is therefore negligible, and is far more than balanced by those lost through the spread of disease made easy by safe travelling everywhere. In addition to this there is a very real loss in virility and keenness. Unbroken peace is no better for Nagas than it is for any other race.'

I find it hard to agree with this. It is true that the suppression of head-hunting, which was closely inter-related with many aspects of Naga culture, will mean an inevitable decay in certain types of dance, personal ornamentation and tattooing, wood-carving and funerary ceremonial. Yet there are more important things than 'culture' and I believe that the greatest gift — and that too the gift most appreciated — which the Administration has brought to NEFA is the gift of peace.

The eyes of the world have been turned so exclusively on the disturbances in Tuensang (caused largely by infiltration from the Naga Hills) that the fundamental changes in other parts of NEFA tend to be forgotten. Yet throughout the area, until very recently, life was disturbed and precarious; in Tirap head-hunting was the order of the day and human sacrifice was not unknown; ferocious inter-village conflicts, kidnapping raids, cruel imprisonments and executions marred the peace of Lohit, Siang and Subansiri; a form of head-hunting among the Mishmis, of hand-hunting among the western Daflas has been recorded. Women and children could not go abroad without an escort and the mists of fear hung heavily above the workers in the fields.

Today all that is changed. Women and children go freely and happily about the countryside, former enemies feast together in amity, communications are open, and the idea of inter-tribal and inter-village co-operation is spreading.

In the classic head-hunting areas of Tirap and Tuensang, war retains its hold on the imagination of the elder men and the warrior is still honoured. He is still honoured also in parts of Siang, where special tombs are made for those who have killed their enemies in battle: one or more gourds cut with holes to represent eyes, nose and mouth, are hung up to symbolize the heads of slaughtered foes.

But the point is that both in Tirap and Tuensang, the people have accepted the idea that head-hunting is against the law, that the days of inter-village wars are over, and that, although friendship and peace may be a little dull, they bring great and lasting benefits. After all, in our own society, we have long since outlawed murder, theft and rape. Yet murders, thefts and rapes occur. But they are the exceptions and not the rule; they are not part of our socially recognized activity. Head-hunting and war are social outlaws today, and this is the great, the almost miraculous, change that has been brought about by the Administration in so short a time. There may well be occasional lapses, but these will not detract from the importance of the main achievement.

Another greatly-treasured gift of the Administration is the lifting of the fear of economic exploitation. There must be few places in the world where such great pains are taken to ensure that 'primitive' people get a square deal. Land is protected, prices are controlled, money-lending is checked, shop-keepers are licenced. The domination of weaker by stronger and more aggressive tribal groups has been ended. The Sherdukpens of Kameng, for example, had previously been taxed not only by Tibetan officials from Tawang, but also by the members of neighbouring tribes. They were frequently raided and had to provide free porterage and supplies to touring officers and the Chiefs of other tribes. The raising of this burden has made a great difference both to their material prosperity and psychological outlook. The Buguns also, who for generations had endured a kind of servitude to the Hrussos, have found a new liberation. The Monpas of Tawang have been freed from excessive taxation from Tibet and the monopolistic exactions of the Drekhang. In many, if not all, parts of NEFA the clouds of fear have been blown away.

But there is an element of truth in Mr Mills' opinion and we must be careful to see that there is no psychological vacuum caused by the disappearance of so absorbing an interest as war.

Suppose that the Great Powers of the world suddenly disbanded all their armed forces and destroyed their weapons, resolved to live at peace with one another. Consider the result of this — the lifting of the burden of fear, the enormous economic gain and consequent release of human energies for scientific and social progress, but at the same time the wide-spread unemployment, the disappearance of the colour and romance of military parades, and possibly the loss of the virile virtues of courage, discipline, physical hardness and the spirit of adventure.

The effect on NEFA has been no less than this. The change-over from a society organized for war to one geared to the arts of peace is bound to have its effect not only on economics, making possible a great advance in agriculture, but even on such matters as the siting of villages (there is no longer any reason for building villages far from the water-supply, on the tops of hills), on dress (which no longer requires to be a sort of armour) and on such arts as carving and the dance, which in some areas were largely inspired by warlike motifs.

In NEFA we are fortunate in having in the Assam Rifles an ideal force, whose men have been described as 'the custodians of law and order, the pioneers of every advance into the interior, the guardians of our borders and, above all, the friends of the hill-people.' Themselves largely recruited from the sub-Himalayan population, they have a natural and instinctive understanding of the NEFA tribesmen, and their approach and conduct is in refreshing contrast to that of the forces of law and order in other parts of tribal India, where for many years I witnessed the devastating psychological and economic effect of the behaviour of the low-grade police.

In some States, to be sent to a tribal area was regarded as a punishment and only policemen who had misbehaved elsewhere were sent there. Far from effective supervision, Sub-Inspectors and constables wrought havoc among the simple tribal people. Corruption, extortion, petty tyranny of every kind, constant demands for free food, free porterage and free labour were the order of the day, and those who should have saved the people from fear were the chief agents in creating it.

Very different is the situation in NEFA, where a tradition of the highest consideration for the tribal people has been established by the Assam Rifles. Here extortion of free food or labour is unthinkable : no one is ever 'framed' for a crime of which he is innocent; even the guilty are treated with kindness and mercy. Modestly, and without fuss, the men of the Assam Rifles have faced every possible hardship and difficulty, and thousands of the wildest of the people think of them with affection and gratitude. May they long continue to be the upholders of the law in the NEFA mountains !

The Problem of Tribal Law

The Administration's attitude to tribal law is one of encouragement and support; it does not interfere in the rulings of the tribal councils unless it has reason to suppose that some serious injustice has been done or a too heavy punishment inflicted. Here it has been fairly successful in working through the local institutions, a very important matter if the vitality of tribal life is to be maintained.

Elsewhere, failure to do this has led in the past to many tragedies and of these I will give one example. In a striking passage, all the more significant because it was written by Englishmen themselves, Thompson and Garratt describe the causes and results of the Santal Rebellion in their *Rise and Fulfilment of British Rule in India.*

'Inside India the Santal rebellion, 1855, at the time was taken as a portent, and aroused much of the alarm and savagery of repression which were to blaze out less than two years later. The Santals, aborigines who in a state of nature live by the chase, a people of extreme simplicity and loveableness, were suffering (as they continue to suffer) from Hindu infiltration.

'This meant change of habits and a whole train of perplexities. Their lands became alienated, they were entangled in debts to people far cleverer than themselves. They were under foolish local officials, who would not help them. The facile reply that the Santals should appeal to the civil courts. or prove their charges of oppression before the criminal courts, was the answer of the father who should offer his son a stone when he asked for bread.

'No one dreamed of insurrection by a race so gentle and harmless, with courts of justice ever open to them; moreover, courts of British justice—which are open to everyone (like the Savoy Hotel). Planters, who were having trouble with the Bengalis praised these "laborious and patient" people; railway contractors delighted in them.

'Then, without warning, a Santal inundation swept over the outlying regions of Bengal, reaching to within a hundred miles of Calcutta, cleaving open skulls of European and Indian alike, pouring out poisoned arrows, burning huts and bungalows. All ended, however, as it was bound to end, in massacre and executions.

'The blood of the martyrs — if we may for a minute forget their wrong-doing and remember only that except by such an outbreak no redress could ever have come to them, for mere grumbling and representation has never brought humanity anything — proved the seed of better conditions. Their land was made into a non-regulation district, and they shared with the Punjab the privilege of exemption from the blessings of justice as dispensed in the law-courts, experiencing in their stead straight-forward protection.'

In other parts of tribal India nothing has been more destructive of the high and simple standards of the tribesmen and their belief in human nature than their relations with the courts and lawyers. Their contact with the ordinary law has led to nervous and moral exhaustion, and the effect of the ordinary processes of the courts has been uniformly bad, even on people who have been in the process of acculturation for a hundred years. I will quote one more opinion by a British administrator (Forsyth); it was written in 1871 of the situation in the Central Provinces, but it may still serve a warning to us today.

'Our administration of civil justice, while perhaps sufficiently suited to the requirements of settled districts, is practically a negation of all justice to the aborigine in his jungle. The courts sit at distant stations; and in the Central Provinces there is even a rule prohibiting the trial of cases by civil officers on tour, unless both parties live on the spot. It wants only the slightest acquaintance with the timid and suspicious aborigine to see that this really amounts to denying him a hearing altogether. He will never come to the station if he can avoid it by any payment within his means to make, and, if he does. the chances are against his succeeding in escaping from it, and the crowd of harpies who clog the wheels of justice, without leaving behind him much of his worldly substance.

'Legislation has never yet enabled an inferior to stand before a superior race; but it has frequently done much to put a weapon in the hands of the aggressors without which the invaded might have held their own.

'The aborigine is the most truthful of beings, and rarely denies either a money obligation or a crime really chargeable against him. When brought into court he will stand on one leg, and holding his ears in his hands in token of submission, freely confess to having battered in a rival's head with his axe. But he has no idea of letters; and so long as his admission of having signed a bond is held to prove against him all the obligations that it may contain, he will continue to be cheated by the man of the pen with whom he deals.

'In fine, our system is too sharp and swift for these people. It is death to the honest, timid and unsettled aboriginal.'

This is not yet a serious problem in NEFA, but we would do well to bear in mind the lessons of history against future developments. The above quotations are, to my mind, a convincing argument in favour of continuing the special arrangements made for the administration of NEFA for many years to come.

A Touch of Healing

Some time ago, the Prime Minister, discussing the hatreds and fears that divide mankind, said that 'a touch of healing' was needed in international relationships. It is this touch of healing which the NEFA Administration hopes to bring to the treatment of crime within its area. Mahatma Gandhi once said what indeed is being accepted by thoughtful people throughout the world:

'All criminals should be treated as patients and a jail should be a hospital for their treatment and cure. No one commits crime for the fun of it. It is a sign of a diseased mind. The causes of the particular disease should be investigated and removed. The outlook of the jail staff should be that of physicians in a hospital. The prisoners should feel that the officials are their friends who are there to help them to regain their mental health and not to harass them in any way'.

This cannot, of course, be the only consideration. It is important, especially in NEFA, to teach respect for the law; tribal people whose idea of social duties has hitherto, in some cases, extended only to their own village or their own tribe, have to realise their obligations to society as a whole; there must be some deterrent against crime; and tribal society itself must feel that justice is done to those who offend against it.

But these aims are to be fulfilled against a background of compassion and understanding of human and tribal needs. A former Chief Justice of India, asked to describe the philosophy which is the basis of modern conceptions of crime and punishment, declared:

'First and foremost it is a philosophy based upon the recognition of human personality because that is the fundamental conception and covers all the rest. It is the feeling that every man, however wicked, however obstinate, however depraved, is nevertheless a human being with rights which he can never forfeit entirely, whatever he has done. Next comes the conception of social justice, that is to say, the claim of the community to protect itself, but with an obligation always to remember that the person against whom it seeks protection is one of its own members and is not to be treated as an outlaw or an outcast. And lastly there is the faith, often shaken but never shattered, in the common humanity of us all, that faith which has so often inspired great saints and prophets but which has scarcely until the present age captured the belief or excited the imagination of the great mass of mankind. I remember very well in the old days, when I heard a judge passing sentence and telling the prisoner, as judges sometimes will, that society must be protected against persons such as he, wondering whether a prisoner would ever ask in his turn, "But who is going to protect me against society?" Society may create criminals as well as punish them, and will continue to do so until it has accepted in full the philosophy of which I have just spoken.'

Such a philosophy, which is so close to the philosophy whereby the NEFA Administration tries to conduct its general affairs, is of special importance in dealing with the tribal offender against the social or legal code. For here concepts of crime, guilt and punishment are very different from those held elsewhere. Some of the NEFA people did in the past imprison captives taken in war or those who broke the tribal rules; a common punishment in Subansiri and western Siang was to put them in the stocks; alternatively they were taken into slavery. There are records of even harsher punishments; the hand that stole was cut off, and in some cases persons were buried alive.

But in general, punishment took the form of fines or compensation. Even murder could be forgiven on payment of a number of mithuns, and the compensation for ordinary theft amounted to two or three times the value of the thing stolen. This had the advantage that Justice was immediately visible and that the injured parties were satisfied that something had been done.

To lock a tribesman up in prison, therefore, is to subject him to an ordeal for which little in his tradition or experience has prepared him. His free and independent spirit suffers not only from incarceration, but also (in the ordinary prisons of the plains) from the unfamiliar food, the difficulty of communication with the staff who are unlikely to know his language, and the unaccustomed heat. When we add to this the fact that such imprisonment brings the hillman, who in many cases has a fundamentally innocent outlook on life, into touch with professional and hardened criminals, as well as political prisoners, the danger is obvious.

Ideas of guilt vary greatly in different societies. To the American Indian, for example, the most important psychological factor is shame rather than a sense of guilt, and the real sanction against crime is the fear of being despised rather than the dread of punishment. This can be so strong that it is said that an Indian, alone in his canoe in the middle of a lake, has been so ashamed at breaking his paddle that he has committed suicide for fear of being ridiculed. In Polynesia, on the other hand, the fundamental sanction is pride, and behaviour is dictated by the approval of the community. In Japan again it is not individual guilt but group guilt that is important. A father will commit suicide because the family has been put to shame, a teacher because his school with a picture of the Emperor has been burnt down. In none of these examples does self-reproachful guilt play a part as it does in Western cultures. Ethics, in fact, can have many different motivations and still remain a powerful force for the direction of human behaviour. We have, therefore, to be careful of what has been called Psychiatric Imperialism, which would mean imposing our own ideas of guilt and punishment on the tribal people.

Pride and self-esteem is a powerful psychological force in NEFA; it is the reason for the great feasts on which men spend the savings of many years, it is behind the impulse to display in a house the horns of every animal sacrificed or killed. The old method of punishment by compensatory fines was thus well founded, for the offender not only suffered materially (and since most of the NEFA people are thoroughgoing materialists, he did not like this), but his pride received a severe blow and he was put to shame. Deprived of his precious mithuns, he was unable to feast his neighbours for many years and his social status was lowered accordingly.

Writers on penal reform have urged that the best way of reforming prisons is to put fewer people in prison. My own view is that we would be wise to send NEFA offenders to jail only in exceptional cases where they are a definite danger to society; and whenever possible to punish them in the traditional way by fine.

But some will have to go to jail, and in order to ensure that the impact of this experience will have the least harmful result, we are establishing a Social Rehabilitation Centre or Sudhar Kendra, as we may perhaps call it, where the touch of healing may be applied to those who have gone astray. We are not going to call it a 'jail' either on the files or in conversation; we will follow the example of Britain's most modern prisons in abolishing such titles as 'Jailor' and 'Warder'. A specially trained officer of rank not less than an A.P.O(I) will be appointed to look after it. He will be assisted by interpreters to ensure free communication, and by craft and agricultural instructors who will fill the days with useful and interesting work. I myself feel it is important that some payment should be made for this work in order to foster the prisoners' self-respect and to enable them to purchase small comforts or send help to their homes.

In Italy jails are set in surrounding of natural beauty, and the NEFA Sudhar Kendra will be built near Lohitpur, where the climate is comparatively good and the people will be among the hills and woods which they love so well. It seems inevitable, under present conditions, to surround the Centre with a high fence for security purposes, but we hope to make the atmosphere and buildings inside this wall as homely and natural as we can. The inmates will live for the most part in long dormitories which will be raised above the ground and have sitting-platforms outside, rather in the manner of the Adi moshup. There will be a community recreation centre, built perhaps like a morung, where the people can sit round a fire and sing. Instead of a bugle it is suggested that there might be a log-drum of the Naga pattern to summon to work or meals.

The food, which will be cooked by the tribal inmates themselves, will be of a kind familiar to them and will include plenty of meat. It is suggested that we should be generous with regard to tobacco and the tribal version of betel, and on special occasions permit even a moderate quantity of rice-bear to be brewed.

Special arrangements will be made for dangerous prisoners, some of whom will be segregated in cells, but there will always be an opportunity for these to be promoted to join the others as a result of good behaviour. Political prisoners will also have to be segregated, and for these too every effort will be made to make the environment homely and even happy. Misery is no foundation for education and progress.

If these and other ideals can be fulfilled, we hope that the Sudhar Kendra will send its inmates back to their hills, restored to mental and social health, to take up their lives again as useful and loyal members of tribal society.

Slavery

Slavery is a heritage from the past which will have to go, and which in fact is already disappearing.

The Government of India is a contracting party to the Slavery Convention of 1926 (though it was only in 1938 that its provisions were applied to NEFA) whereby it agreed to bring about progressively and as soon as possible the disappearance of slavery in every form. The British Government, while doing all it could by persuasion to achieve this, took the line that it was impracticable to enforce anti-slavery provisions in areas that were not under full administration. It gave shelter, however, to slaves who escaped into settled territory and occasionally even paid compensation for them. Before Independence, however, progress was very slow, except among the Minyongs of Siang, where slavery was completely eliminated.

What is a slave? He is someone who is the property of another person and entirely subject to him. He has to live with and work for someone else, often (at least at first) against his will. His children will have the same fate and they, like him, can be bought and sold.

Slaves became slaves for a number of reasons. They were captured in war. They were purchased. They were used to repay a debt. Many were born slaves. Sometimes a man became a slave because he had committed a serious offence against the community and could not afford the fine demanded.

Slavery in the fullest sense of the word has existed from time immemorial in NEFA, but it is somewhat different from what once was practiced in the west. In the first place, it is on a comparatively small scale. It is estimated that some millions of slaves were imported into America during the period of the African slave-trade. In the whole of NEFA there are only a few thousand slaves, many of them in the lightly administered areas. Ten years ago, the slave population of the Lohit Valley was not more than two hundred.

Secondly, there is no racialism in NEFA slavery. Western slavery took a darker tinge from the prevailing theory of the racial inequality of the slaves. Negroes, it was held, were only part human; by becoming slaves they were expiating the sins of their fathers; they did not deserve the elementary human rights; even a freed slave was irrevocably an inferior being. Yet many of the American slaves were in practice well-treated as members of the family, and one of the arguments used by the anti-Abolitionists was that the Negroes *liked* being slaves and would only be unhappy if they were liberated.

In NEFA too slaves often win a good position in their masters' homes, and naturally, after a period of years, come to be accepted as members of the family. The owner provides his slave with food, clothing and shelter; he arranges his marriage and pays the bride-price. In some areas a slave is allowed to keep part of any earnings he may receive.

But, as in America, there is a strong taboo on social and sexual relations between slave and free. As in America, there is an emphatic belief in the social inferiority of slaves, and even a freed slave, though he may become headman of his village, is forever barred from marriage with a girl of a free family. The status of a slave is suggested by the use of such words as 'dog' or 'fowl' to describe him — a dog or a fowl is something that is entirely in your power; you can sell or otherwise dispose of it as you will.

A slave by definition is something that can be bought and sold. Many NEFA slaves have been, and still are, used as merchandize, and in the course of a lifetime may be bought and sold a dozen times. It is thus incorrect to say that there is no real slavery in NEFA and that the slaves should be called serfs.

It is true that slaves may, in many places, ransom themselves if they can find the necessary money. There is already a movement, inspired by the liberal ideas of human brotherhood spread by the Administration, for slaves to demand their freedom; they are trying to escape in greater numbers than formerly, and some slave-owners are seriously perturbed about the situation. The matter is complicated by the fact that a number of tribal employees, such as Political Jamadars, and headmen who are recognized by Government, themselves keep slaves, sometimes on a rather large scale.

Since Independence, in areas which are fully administered, our officers have had as their aim the ending of all traffic in slaves, while the capture of persons for the extortion of ransom is regarded as a serious matter. Money has been sanctioned for the payment of compensation to slave-owners, for were no compensation to be paid, there would be considerable social and economic dislocation.

In some places the slave-owners take a businesslike attitude to the subject, and provided compensation is paid to make up for their initial outlay, are quite willing to release their slaves. In the past, for various reasons, there has been a certain reluctance on the part of our officers to spend the money allocated for this purpose; but I believe that if more money were to be spent, we might be able to solve this great human problem more expeditiously.

On the other hand, it is important that we should not create political resentment in areas where we are not yet in sufficient authority to enforce our decisions. The task of liberation is proceeding steadily; it is considered wise, now that the worse features of the institution have been eliminated, to allow it to proceed slowly. It must be remembered that every individual liberation is a delicate matter, demanding the attention of a responsible officer who has to conduct complicated financial arrangements. In the last four years, 79 slaves have been liberated in the Subansiri Division, 10 in Siang and 32 in Lohit. In some cases a liberated slave has continued to work for his former master with a new status, of his own free will. In other cases, the slaves have been helped to find a livelihood and settle down as free members of society.

During the last four years, there has not been a single case recorded of any new slave being captured or purchased in the fully administered area, and the traffic in slaves across the border of Tibet and Burma has been almost entirely checked.

Nothing will illustrate the realities of slavery in NEFA better than the following history of a Tagin slave-woman who has recently been liberated in the Bori area in the Siang Frontier Division.

The Story of Yaniyong

Yaniyong was born in a Tagin village, Neli-Daring, and had two sisters and three brothers. When she was six years old she was betrothed and went to her husband's house when she was still very young. She had three daughters, of whom two died in infancy. One day when her youngest daughter was about four years old, she had a dream that a bird flew up into the sky and perched on one of the great swings that are erected to appease the Wiyu (demon) of dysentry and on which a number of boys were playing. Some people came by dragging a mithun by a rope. Yaniyong understood this dream to mean that her husband would die, that her village would be raided and that she herself would be dragged away like a captive mithun.

After some time her father-in-law had a quarrel with another Tagin, from Dollung village, and killed him. A little while afterwards the Dollung people came to take revenge. On the way they met Yaniyong's husband who had gone to the forest to collect leaves and killed him. They came into the village and, though Yaniyong's father-in-law and the rest of the family managed to escape into the forest, she herself (who was carrying her baby on her back) and her husband's younger sister were captured.

As they were being dragged away Yaniyong, who after all was still very young, sat on the ground refusing to move. But her enemies pulled her up by her necklaces and broke them. Then they tied her hands together and dragged her along, threatening to kill her until at last in despair she went quietly. Her husband's younger sister, however, caused her captors so much trouble that half-way along the path they murdered her.

When Yaniyong reached Dollung she was put in the stocks, but only one foot was fastened because she had her baby and her enemies felt rather sorry for her. Otherwise, she says, she was well-treated and given the same food as her captors had. At first when she was being taken away from her own village she was full of spirit, furious with the other villagers for not rescuing her, and full of plans for escape. But once she had been put in the stocks she only had one thought and that was to save her life, no matter what kind of life that would be. The Tagins kept her in the stocks for three days and then took her to a Gallong village called Yamsa to sell her as a slave, for they were afraid that she would run away or her clansmen would come and rescue her. Accordingly, when they took her to Yamsa they took her by a very round-about path so that she would not be able to find her way back and this took four days. The Dollung people were paid a mithun for Yaniyong herself and various small things for the baby.

Yaniyong remained a month in Yamsa and during that time her baby died. She recalls that she did not feel any particular shame at having become a slave, but she felt very lonely. To this of course was added the sorrow for the loss of her baby, whose death was probably hastened by the fact that she was given very bad food and made to work extremely hard. There was no one to look after the child and so she had to carry her all the time on her back. When the baby fell ill her master refused to make any sacrifices for her. When the child died Yaniyong herself had to dig the grave and carry the little body for burial. Not one of the Gallongs was willing to help her. She had been warned that this might happen by a dream in which she saw herself throwing her clothes into a hole in the ground which she had made in the hope of getting water.

When the child died the Yamsa people thought that it would be now easy for Yaniyong to make her escape and they took her accordingly to Yanking village.

Yaniyong's price had now risen and the Yamsa people demanded three mithuns for her. In the house of the man at Yanking where they hoped to sell her, there were already two other slaves and they pressed their owner to buy her because she could then be given to one of them as a wife, but he considered that the price was too high and only kept Yaniyong in the house, on approval as it were, for three days. He finally decided not to have her and the Yamsa people took her from village to village trying to sell her. They went to the Bori villages of Mega, Boga and Gameng and in Gameng a man bought her for two bronze pots, which were considered to be the equivalent of four mithuns.

When she was in Gameng, Yaniyong began to realise what it meant to be a slave and felt so ashamed that she would not speak to anyone : she used to sit in a corner hiding her face in her hands. But after she reached Gameng she decided that after all she was alive and was getting food and shelter and that she might as well make the best of things. She began to work well and recalls that she was not unhappy.

But after about a year the wife of the house began to give Yaniyong a great deal of trouble. She did not feed her properly and continually abused her : 'Wife of a monkey', 'Wife of a bear', 'Wife of a dog'. 'Wife of a cock', and this used to upset her so much that she thought : 'Let me die but not live like this'. After a time, however, Yaniyong began to answer back and made life so unpleasant that her owner decided to sell her. He took her first to Gasheng, where he failed to find a purchaser, and then to Gatte. There one Tada Pangu bought her for three bronze dishes and one mithun. These three dishes were not old and valuable ones and were considered to be worth only about fifty rupees each.

After a time, however, Tada married his daughter to a man in Gasheng and sent Yaniyong with her as a servant. While she was there the Boris offered a human sacrifice to check an epidemic of dysentry and Yaniyong along with the others swallowed a piece of human flesh. But she was so revolted that she brought it up immediately.

Now in Gasheng there was a young widower called Tapung Pabing (Yaniyong was living in the house of a member of the Pabing clan). Although he was a freeman he fell in love with Yaniyong, who was very beautiful. When his clansmen discovered this they threatened to turn him out of the village and beat him for lowering the credit of their clan. Tapung explained the situation to Yaniyong and said that in any case he was in great danger : he would be killed either in the village or, if he ran away, he would die in the forest. Yaniyong then proposed that they should run away together. So the two lovers, saying that they were going to work in the fields, quietly slipped away into the forest and, avoiding the regular tracks, made their way over the wild and desolate mountains for four days until they reached Pangkang. From there they went on to Karko. There they found service, but not of course as slaves, in a Minyong house and gradually built a house for themselves.

Shortly before the elopement Yaniyong had a dream that she had gone down into a hole in the ground and had travelled under the earth in darkness for many weary years until at last she came out into a place of light, where she saw Doini-Pollo, the Supreme Being, in his beauty. This is surely a fine symbol of a woman's escape from slavery into the light of freedom.

One day Tapik Pangu, the brother of Yaniyong's former owner at Gatte, came to Karko and abused Tapung for having carried off a slave-girl. To this Tapung replied that as Tapik was a Pangu and had given the girl to the Pabing clan, it was no business of his what a member of another clan did. Tapik held a Kebang (council) but was unable to do anything and went away. While Yaniyong was at Karko the great earthquake occurred and this fixes the date of her stay there as 1950.

After a time Yaniyong and her husband left Karko and went to the Bori village of Paying where they made a house and settled down. After a time, however, Tapung fell ill with what may have been some kind of liver trouble. They called the priests and offered as many sacrifices as they could afford but to no effect. They went to Along for treatment but were asked to go down to Pasighat. Tapung remained in the Pasighat hospital for a month but did not get better and so finally the couple went back to Paying.

Tapung's younger brother was living in Mega and Tapung thought that if he could be with one of his own relations he would get the help he needed. In Mega Tapung himself was looked after well and given good food, but his relatives did not like Yaniyong — who was after all a Tagin while they were Boris — and his brother's wife used constantly to abuse her as a slave girl and a bitch and refused to give her the same food as her husband. Yaniyong did not mind this particularly, but her husband resented it and said, 'I am not going to die in this house. Let me die in a Taring household and the Taring people will sacrifice a pig at my death and will provide cloth for my burial. When I am dead my wife will work for them and they will look after her.' A Kebang was held and Tapung was taken to a house of the Taring clan. On that very day, shortly after he reached his new home, he died. The Taring people did all that was required; one of them carried the body out for burial, they dug the grave, sacrificed a pig and provided cloth for the corpse.

After her husband's death Yaniyong stayed in the house of the Taring people and worked for them, but not as a slave. She recalls that she had no trouble at that time except her natural sorrow for the loss of her husband. The one thing that consoled her was that she was free. But one day she dreamt that her father had gone to a certain village and bought a mithun. When he tied the rope round the animal's neck he found that it was not an animal but a man, and he dragged the man back to his village. Soon afterwards Tapik Pangu came to Mega and declared, 'This woman was my father's elder brother's slave and now belongs to me. The old man had sent this girl to Gasheng to look after his daughter and she ran away from there, but she really belongs to me and I am going to take her back.' The Taring people protested at this, saying that Tapung had entrusted Yaniyong to their care and they had performed all the business for the funeral. If Tapik wanted to take the girl away, they said, he would have to refund their expenses. Tapik finally gave a bronze dish (worth about twenty-five rupees), a cooking-pot worth about fifteen rupees, two rupees in cash and three seers of salt and for this trivial sum Yaniyong was sent back to slavery.

When Yaniyong was taken away she was filled with despair and wanted to die. Her husband was dead and she was once more a slave, so what was the use of going on living?

Yaniyong stayed in Gatte for some time and then met Tage Pangu, a freed Tagin slave of Gasheng. He is a small and cheerful person, a very typical Tagin and apparently had some sort of affair with Yaniyong when she had been in Gasheng some years before. Yaniyong disliked Gatte and with the added attraction of Tage, became very anxious to go and live in Gasheng.

So one day Yaniyong went to Gasheng to the headman, Tarang Pabing, and told him how much she disliked Gatte and begged him to purchase her, promising to work for him in his house.

Tarang was not at first willing to do this but Yaniyong pressed him strongly and in the end he purchased her for one bronze pot said to be worth two mithuns, beads worth one mithun and a Tibetan coat. But later, Tarang became afraid that he might get into trouble with Government and when I myself visited the village, hurriedly demanded the things he had paid to Tapik and asked him to take Yaniyong back to his house.

From Gasheng, I brought Yaniyong with my party on the long journey to Along Directly the Political Officer heard her story, he set in train measures for her liberation. Within a fortnight, as a result of the energy and tact of our interpreters, under the wise guidance of the P.O., Yaniyong was freed and entered into tne world of light and beauty of the free.

I have told this story at length for it shows in a vivid way what life in NEFA once was like, and it is surely an inspiration to all our officers. This is one of the most romantic and worth-while of the many opportunities for service facing us in NEFA, and we may confidently look forward to the day, in the not too distant future, when the whole of NEFA will — to use a famous phrase of the old anti-slavery movement — 'be consecrated by the genius of universal emancipation'.

Opium

The taking of opium, which under the tolerant laissez-faire policy of the former regime, gained almost a stranglehold over certain tribes, is another custom in which Government obviously has to interfere.

For its curse lies heavily on the border villages. It is an astonishing experience to travel along the Patkoi Range from Raho to Havi and see the fields of poppy usurping food-crops in the jhums and the little opium-gardens behind almost every house. Without seeing it, it is not easy to imagine the extent of this cultivation, the energy expended on it and the care with which it is cherished. Opium is almost a form of currency; it may form part of a girl's bride-price; it may be used to pay a fine; it is perhaps the most valuable of all tribal products for export or local trade. Some villages, like Wakka, grow opium solely for business : its hardy virile men scorn its enervating pleasures; but they grow it on a fairly large scale for their weaker neighbours.

It was agreed everywhere that opium-addiction was on the increase; it is now taken in the morungs, where the young men have no longer to be alert in the new era of peace. Dr R. N. Chopra, who is our chief authority on opium addiction in India, found among patients examined by him that the habit had been contracted in 50% of the cases by association with other smokers for its euphoric effects, in 33% for relief of pain and sickness, and in 17% to overcome worry and nerve-strain. The people with whom I discussed the matter laid chief emphasis on the spread of the habit through imitation : a group would be sitting round the fire, and one or two of the older men would have their pipes. It was only natural that the younger men should have a try, and having tried to be seduced by the pleasurable effect.

I think, however, that the cold and gloom of the climate must play its part, and it is significant that the highest incidence of opium-smoking occurs in those tribal groups whose culture is in the greatest state of decay. Life is dull, hard and boring, and the pipe offers all too easy an escape into a land of dreams.

Efforts have already been made, especially in the Singpho area and in the Borduria villages, to wean the people from the habit and some success has been achieved. But the time has come for a determined and comprehensive programme to bring this evil to an end throughout NEFA.

The fear is sometimes expressed that vigorous action may have political repercussions. There was also the danger of political repercussions when head-hunting was stopped. But, in my opinion, opium-addiction is a greater evil even than head-hunting, which did not in practice lead to the loss of many lives (it is recorded, for example, that during sixteen years, in which two villages were in a constant state of war, only four heads were taken). Head-hunting fostered the martial virtues, it maintained a high degree of discipline, it was the inspiration of carving and weaving, the dance and song. But opium is the destruction of all these things. No art can flourish, no virtue or discipline can be maintained, no plans for development will be successful so long as this problem remains unsolved. The Noctes, Konyaks and Mishmis addicted to opium are poor, thin, miserable, caught in a vicious circle so that the poorer they grow the more they turn to opium for relief, and the more they smoke the poorer they become.

At one time the British tried to solve the problem by wholesale destruction of the poppy-crop wherever it was found. This will not lead to success today. A comprehensive plan is being drawn up by NEFA's Medical Department which will include propaganda, treatment where possible, gradual elimination of poppy-cultivation, permission to smoke only by licence and the restriction of such licences only to proved addicts of a certain age, and above all by a vigorous positive programme to bring prosperity and happiness to the afflicted villages, so that a new interest may drive out the old.

Alcohol

Alcohol is in a very different category. Some form of rice or millet beer holds an important place in the esteem of all the tribes. It is an essential element in the tradition of hospitality which is one of the most admired of tribal virtues; it is an important element in the price paid for a bride; it is almost a medium of exchange; it has its share in most religious rituals; no tribal conference can succeed without it; it is the cement that binds together those who make a pact of peace.

But, in my experience, the NEFA tribals rarely drink to excess. They do not booze regularly as the tribesmen of Madhya Pradesh do, and in all my tours I have rarely seen a drunken man. Rice-beer is a food and, if it is to be taken in excess at all, it should be on some occasion of crisis or rejoicing — a wedding or a funeral, a harvest festival or (in former days) a victory over one's foes.

The Administration, while being tolerant of homemade rice-beer, has rightly set its face against the distillation of spirit. The only place where I have found a little drunkenness is among the Sherdukpens and Monpas and they use a very potent rice-spirit. In Madhya Pradesh distilled spirit has been a curse to the tribesmen in a way that the more gentle palm-wine and rice-beer has never been. Nor has it the food-values of the more natural drinks. This is a matter which needs careful watching.

For the promotion of temperance in NEFA, the popularization of tea will be very useful. This beverage is already acceptable to many tribes, and on tour I found that tea-leaves were one of the most useful of all presents.

A rather special problem arises over the taking of alcohol by officers. We have no prohibition in NEFA, but it is most important that members of the staff should not drink too much and, at all costs, never get actually drunk. Nothing lowers the prestige of an officer more in tribal eyes than this, and there is a further danger that he may lose control of himself and speak in an abusive manner or even strike someone — a thing that is not readily forgiven. Indeed there is a local tradition that one of the great tragedies of long ago, which cost the lives of some valuable officers and led to a punitive expedition which, it is popularly believed, brought malaria and syphilis into the hills, was due to an officer losing control of himself when drunk and striking an influential Chief. One act of excess had incalculable consequences and is still remembered.

The problem is the more difficult because in NEFA the temptations to drink are many There is the sunless, cold and hostile climate; there is the nervous strain of sometimes having to work, without chance of relaxation in other company, with people one may dislike; there are the discouragements and anxieties incidental to all human life but here accentuated by distance and isolation. There are various ways of overcoming these temptations but, especially for a young officer, the most dangerous is the bottle.

Yet another temptation comes from the people themselves. They are very hospitable and often press large quantities of rice-beer on visitors. What should an officer do when he is offered this? If he is not a teetotaller and has a strong stomach, he may accept in moderation. If he is a teetotaller, he may well follow the example of the former Governor, Shri Jairamdas Daulatram, and raise any drink offered him to his lips to show that he has no taboo in his mind and as a symbol of unity with his hosts. The Administration has advised its officers along these lines.

It has been urged that if we do not drink, we shall cause offense. It has also been urged that in actual fact our refusal will not really be resented. I think that the danger of giving offense has certainly been exaggerated, but that is not really the point. The danger is not so much that we will offend the people as that we will create a feeling that we are alien to them. We should never, for example, say: 'It is against my custom or religion to take alcohol.' In Kohima in 1955 Shri Phizo made capital out of the fact that a feast of pork and rice-beer offered to a distinguished Hindu visitor had not been acceptable. 'Here', said Phizo, 'is a symbol of the unbridgeable gap between Nagaland and India'.

The Problem of Time

It is not going to be easy for a comparatively small population to find sufficient working-hours in the year to fulfil all the demands that we are making upon it. This problem is already exercising some of the more thoughtful villagers in all Divisions. We call the people for porterage, for road-making, for the construction and repair of bridges, to build official quarters. We ask them to send boys and girls, who would ordinarily be working in the fields, to schools, to the CITPC's, to National Volunteer Camps, to enlist in the Army, to tour round India. We engage some of them as domestic servants or as Class IV officials or in the A.S.C. We frequently summon the headmen to headquarters, often from very distant places, on official business, for special occasions and to meet VIP's. Every officer who visits a village on tour distracts the people from their ordinary work; we now have Research Officers who will require the elders to spend long hours giving them information: we propose to engage the people to make recordings for broadcasts and pose before the camera for documentary films. And the burden of all this falls inevitably on the most enterprising and intelligent. Where, I have often been asked on tour, are we to find time for the agriculture which you tell us is our fundamental need?

I do not know what the solution of this problem is, but it is one that we should consider very seriously. A partial solution, however, could be reached if it were possible to eliminate from tribal life some of the ways whereby the people waste their time. The system of gennas or taboos, for example, involves a tragic waste of man-hours, for throughout the year on every conceivable occasion the people are forbidden to work in the fields or go out of their villages. The present system of marriage is another great consumer of time, for a number of expeditions have to be made to a bride's house with appropriate gifts before the marriage is complete. The Adis spend a quite disproportionate amount of their time in litigation; they are mighty talkers (the Boris say that an orator should have a tongue four yards long) and the proceedings of the Kebangs are dragged on for hours. The many days lost as a result of long journeys to buy salt and other necessities will, of course, gradually be saved as we make it possible for the tribesmen to buy their goods from local Government shops. Sickness is another enemy of time, for an attack of fever, which elsewhere would only incapacitate the invalid, in NEFA diverts an entire household, as well as priests and village elders, to the longdrawn ritual of appeasement of the deities of disease. What a doctor will do in ten minutes may take a tribal physician three days.

Formerly, none of this mattered very much, for the tribal people had plenty of time, and it provided an interest in life and filled up hours which might otherwise have been spent less profitably. But today, if the ideals and plans of the Second Five-Year Plan are to be implemented, everybody in NEFA will have to be on his toes, and there will not be a moment to waste. We must mobilize our manpower and get the utmost possible amount of work out of everyone.

The anthropologists would violently oppose me in this, but I have come to the conclusion that somehow or other, while preserving our respect for tribal institutions and continuing to follow our policy of not imposing our ways upon the tribal people, we must try to weaken the hold of the genna-taboo, to shorten the work of the priest and shaman, and to discourage the habit of litigation. This can only be done gradually, and with the greatest care, but something of the kind will have to come about if the people are to fit in to the new order.

Other Problems

In addition to these fundamental problems, there are others about which there is room for a difference of opinion, but with which, on the whole, it would be wise not to interfere. It will be a different matter if and when the people themselves wish to change, but we should neither encourage nor discourage this. Let us sometimes realise that there are things which are just not our business. We are not in NEFA as reformers, and the Prime Minister himself has deprecated the attitude that wishes to go about doing good.

There are two characters in the novels of Charles Dickens whom we would do well to study. One is Mrs Pardiggle in *Bleak House*, the embodiment of 'rapacious benevolence'. She is 'businesslike and systematic': she has a 'mechanical way of taking possession of people'; she specialises in 'a knowledge of the poor' and a capacity for doing 'charitable business in general'; she makes 'a great show of moral determination'. And when she visits a bricklayer's house like 'an inexorable moral policeman' and lectures him on architecture, sanitation and 'improvement', the poor victim exclaims: 'I want an end of these liberties took with my place.'

A similar character is Mr Pumblechook, in *Great Expectations*, who could never see a small boy without trying to improve him by setting him problems in mental arithmetic. And I have little doubt that faced by the all too common self-conscious desire to uplift one's fellows, that hard professional inquisitive interference in other peoples' lives so characteristic of the social worker, tribal India's reaction is: 'I want an end of the liberties taken with my place'.

One of these problems concerns the dormitory, which exists among certain Naga groups, among the Sherdukpens and very widely in Siang. In the Minyong, Padam and Bori villages, for example, there are dormitories for the boys (*dere* or *moshup*) and girls (*rasheng*) which have the useful purpose of disciplining the youth of the tribe, promoting song and dance, and organizing the boys and girls for various community services.

It has been reported from the Pasighat area that in a few villages this system is now breaking down under the influence of the local schools. School-boys and dormitory-boys are known by different names and are growing into opposition to each other. Similarly in Tuensang, the morung-boys are often opposed to the Christian boys. We are now trying to change this and to make the schools and dormitories not rivals but allies. For disappearance of the dormitories would mean, as it has meant when they have disappeared in similar cultures elsewhere, a general weakening of tribal discipline, a decay of the recreational arts and an increase of sexual promiscuity.

It is argued, however, that since sometimes the boys visit the girls' dormitories, the system contributes to the spread of venereal disease.

The incidence of venereal disease, invariably syphilis, in NEFA is disquieting, but it is not noticeably higher among the groups that have the dormitory. The Singphos and certain Konyaks, the Apa Tanis, and the Monpas of Kameng, all of whom suffer from this disease, do not have the girl's dormitory. In most tribal cultures, indeed, the dormitory acts as a check against infection by segregating and disciplining the young girls of the community. Where all the unmarried girls sleep together in one place under some sort of communal discipline, it is very difficult for one of them to spend a night or even a few hours of the night away from the others; where girls are scattered in their own homes, or in little groups, about the village, it is obviously easier for an outsider who wishes to misbehave with one of them to do so. The dormitory is the guardian of tribal endogamy.

Most of the tribes, whether they have the dormitory or not, allow a good deal of premarital sexual freedom to the young; at the same time they insist on a high standard of marital fidelity. I do not think that to close the girls' dormitories would promote conventional morality; it would merely drive the natural and simple freedom underground. To forbid the dormitory would create a sense of guilt, but would not change the standards of conduct — and that cannot be a good thing.

A special and difficult problem is the high price of wives. There is a marked inflation in the NEFA marriage-market, inevitable where bride-price is usually paid in kind. Twenty years ago, six mithuns did not represent a very large sum of money; today they do. The coming of a money-economy to NEFA may make it difficult for the sons of poorer families to obtain suitable wives, with a consequent lowering of moral standards.

Girls also sometimes find it difficult to obtain suitable husbands. This is specially so among the Gallongs of Siang, where a peculiar system of betrothal and marriage often results in mature girls being married to baby boys. This is favourable neither to morality nor happiness, and I think that possibly we might, very tactfully, try to inspire the Gallongs to modify this custom and in fact some of their leaders are already doing so. We might also try to lower the bride-price where possible.

The Problem of Intermarriage

With this is closely associated the problem of inter-marriage of members of the NEFA staff with tribal girls.

At first sight, this may seem to be a thing to be encouraged — we aim at unity with the tribes and there can be no greater unity than this. There have been a number of exceptionally happy unions between tribal wives and non-tribal husbands, just as there have been many happy inter-national and inter-caste marriages. These have undoubtedly done something to break down racial and social barriers.

On the other hand, tribal communities everywhere, and especially those at the stage of social development represented in NEFA, are what the anthropologists call endogamous, and the people look with disfavour on any sexual or marital relation either with non-tribals or members of other tribes. Tribal marriage is further regulated by rules of class, clan and relationship, and fidelity to these rules is regarded as one of the fundamental principles of tribal discipline, and as one of the chief means of preserving the purity and continuity of the race.

We are pledged to respect the customs and manners of the tribal people, and they would certainly give the law of endogamy high priority in any list of customs they wished preserved.

We are also pledged to respect tribal religion and, as officers of a secular democracy, we are not to attempt to change that religion or interfere in it any way. The effect of marriage with a non-tribal, however, is almost always to cause the tribal partner to change her religion, her name, and her entire way of life. This may in time, especially if it occurs on a large scale, cause various difficulties and complications.

For there would be no very serious problem if there were not so many of us. A number of new officials, many of them young and unmarried, will be coming into NEFA in the next few years. There is a risk that the tribal people will grow apprehensive that their best girls are going to be taken away from them as wives of members of the staff, and this may easily lead to political resentment.

A more personal and human problem concerns the happiness and future of the tribal girl who marries an outsider. In some cases such marriages have turned out uncommonly well, but this has not always been so. There is perhaps no difficulty in the early years when a girl's non-tribal husband is stationed in her own country, among her own people. But suppose her husband is transferred to another station; suppose his parents and relatives strongly disapprove of the marriage; suppose he resigns and returns home to live in a town. The lot of a hill-girl in an unfriendly alien atmosphere in the unfamiliar urban setting of the plains may not be a very happy one.

If inter-marriage with the tribals become too common, there is a danger of the present very happy relations between the staff and the people being disturbed; the simple and natural behaviour of tribal women may change and a kind of purdah may be started. For example, some tribes in central India have deliberately made their women ugly (by tattooing their faces) so as to render them unattractive to outsiders.

Whenever, therefore, there is any question of a member of the staff wishing to marry a tribal girl, we have asked our senior men to keep these general principles in mind and to explain them carefully to the officer concerned. We should remember that this can be a very critical moment in a young man's life, and we should give friendly, almost paternal, guidance. We must face the fact that some of the younger men, in the vigour of their youth, in their isolation, boredom and loneliness, have to struggle with great temptations and they need our help. If the problem is approached rationally and tactfully, a senior officer may often be able to convince a young recruit that marriage with a tribal girl may not, in the long run, be for the greatest happiness of either party and may involve practical difficulties which make it undesirable.

The Administration has now decided, however, that in some exceptional cases a Political Officer, having discussed the matter fully with the officer concerned, may approve of such a marriage provided that he is convinced that both parties to it are sincerely in love with each other; that the officer intends to make NEFA his lifework and that there is a reasonable chance of the marriage being permanent; that the girl's relatives approve; and that the normal tribal formalities are observed and the bride-price paid.

In a word, therefore, inter-marriage is not to be encouraged but may, in certain circumstances, be allowed.

It is obvious that this policy will demand sacrifices from some members of the staff, yet it has been adopted both in the interest of the people themselves and to ensure the highest possible standard of conduct.

The Disposal of the Dead

Another problem concerns the method of disposing of the dead by exposure — a practice which some younger officers in their enthusiasm have tried to stop. Indeed, some villages are under the impression, wrongly, that it has been forbidden by the Administration.

The custom of exposing the dead is widespread. Certain Kshattriya clans practiced it in ancient India; the Parsis maintain it to this day. It has been recorded from Melanesia and Madagascar. It exists only in a comparatively small area of NEFA. Professor Hutton has drawn a distinction between the Western Nagas (the Angamis, Semas, Rengmas, Lhotas and Tangkhuls), all of whom bury their dead, and the central Nagas, such as the Aos, the Konyak tribes and the Khienmungans, who expose them. Rich Aos, for example, until fairly recently, kept a corpse in the outer room of a house and lit a fire beneath it until it was smoke-dried. At the next Harvest Festival it was laid on a platform erected beside a path outside the village. If this was not done, the relations were told that they had not given the dead man his due of loving attention. But gradually under the influence of education the custom of keeping the bodies in the houses passed, and now even the practice of exposing bodies outside has largely been abandoned by the Aos, who have taken to burying the dead like the Western Nagas.

It is probable that just as the Aos have changed, the Konyaks, Phoms and Khienmungans will change in time, and they will ultimately either cremate or bury their dead. But it is surely better that they should do this of their own accord; already some educated Konyaks, for example, are trying to influence their people in this direction. For to interfere with death customs is always unwise. Tribal people are extraordinarily sensitive to everything connected with this subject. They believe that the spirits of the dead have power over the living, that they can ruin the harvest and kill the child in the womb, and it is thus essential not to irritate them by failing to perform the prescribed rituals.

Among some tribes there is the custom of burying the dead beside the house or even (as among some of the Tangsas) beneath it: this is partly to protect the corpse from being desecrated by wild animals, partly to keep the ghost in the warmth and shelter of his former home. Some junior officers have rebuked the people for this practice. This is most unwise.

In western Kameng, and indeed in places all along the northern frontier the people follow the Tibetan practice of cutting up a dead body and throwing it into a river. This custom, however repugnant to some of us, should never be criticized.

The danger of any interference in funerary customs is illustrated by the tragic example of the Ninu Massacre.

On the 1st of February 1875, two British officers attached to the Topographical Survey, Captain Badgley and Lieutenant Holcombe, arrived with their escort at Ninu. The tragic incidents that then befell and the ferocious retaliation that they excited are fully described in the General Reports of the Topographical Surveys of India for 1874-75, published in Calcutta in 1876. The Wanchos of Ninu attacked and slaughtered Holcombe and many of his troops in what appeared to the survivors an inexplicable act of treachery. No reason for the massacre is given in any of the official reports and it seem to have been assumed that it was a natural reaction of tribal savagery to the march of civilization. The punitive expeditions that quickly followed destroyed several villages.

When I camped at Ninu (I stayed in the Chief's morung), I was naturally interested to discover whether the people had any recollection of the events of eighty years ago, and it was soon evident that not only had they lively traditions of them, but they had suffered emotional and psychological wounds that were still unhealed. The account given by the Chief and other elders agreed more or less with the official reports so far as the general course of events was concerned, but they added the reason for the massacre about which our records have hitherto been silent.

According to Ninu tradition, the British officers and their escort camped at a little distance from the village. Only a week before, the Chief had died and the usual elaborate tomb had been built with a carved wooden effigy before it. Shortly after their arrival some of the troops, who were described as Nepalese, went into the village and saw the Chief's tomb. They laughed at it and one of them struck the effigy with his cane, and they abused the people for disposing of their dead in the way they did. There were three men from Borduria who had accompanied the military party and these seem to have acted as interpreters. In the evening, the Ninu people, full of rage at the insult to their dead Chief and to their customs, and further inflamed (it was said) by the men from Borduria, decided to take revenge and next morning they surrounded the camp and killed Holcombe with some eighty of his men.

No New Taboos

There is a final and most important point. Not only are we not to interfere in tribal social life and custom unless there is something which offends against law and order or the universal conscience of mankind, but we are equally not to introduce harmful customs and ideas from our own society.

One of these, to which I have already referred, is the drinking of spirits as against rice-beer; another is gambling with cards. In Lohit I found many Idus playing a curious mixture of bridge and whist, which they had been taught by A.S.C. porters. I once timed a group of boys engaged in this profitable exercise. They played steadily for five-and-a-half hours during the morning and for three hours again at night. I remember too how some time ago I saw Ao youths, splendid healthy active boys, spending the best part of a morning round the carrom board. The introduction of 'civilized' diversions is not always for the benefit of the tribal people.

We have also to be cautious that we do not import into NEFA our own system of taboos. I have spoken elsewhere of the extreme sensitivity of the people to any interference in their habits of food and drink. We must never give the impression that we look down on anyone for eating beef — or for that matter snakes and monkeys. If the matter ever comes up we may well mention that the most civilized people in the world, the French, eat snails and frogs. Great offence was once caused at one of our training-centres when the officer in charge abused the Mishmi and Adi boys there as 'jungly', 'beef-eaters' and 'monkey-eaters'.

Most important of all is the danger of introducing a caste system among the NEFA people. Some of the tribal groups have a sort of class system : for example, the Konyaks and Wanchos have three sharply defined classes, between which inter-marriage is at least theoretically forbidden; the Sherdukpens and Buguns have a two-class system; the freed slaves of Siang are forming a class above the slaves but below and separate from the rest of the population.

But there has never been anything like real caste or untouchability in NEFA, and it is a point sometimes made by missionary and N.N.C. propaganda that we may bring this and other inequitable ideas into the hills.

And if we introduce sweepers into NEFA, who can deny that they may be right? Untouchability has been outlawed and not one of our senior officers would touch it even in thought. But there are a sufficient number of the subordinate staff as well as contractors, shop-keepers, road-labourers and others who undoubtedly still look, and are likely to look for many years to come, on the sweepers as a lower type of human being, and they may infect the tribals with the same opinion. In central India, a strong feeling of repulsion towards the sweeper, the leather-worker and the blacksmith has developed among the tribal people as a result of contact with civilization during the last few decades.

Even to bring in sweepers from outside, therefore, is likely to have a bad effect; to employ tribals as sweepers and to lay the foundations of a tribal sweeper caste or submerged sub-clan would be a real crime against the people. Some Kabui Nagas have taken up the work of sweepers in Imphal town and this is greatly resented by other Nagas. They are already a class apart and are banned from marriage and interdining with their fellows. In NEFA too a few tribal sweepers have in the past been employed and have been promptly excommunicated by their fellows.

The Administration has, therefore, ordered that no sweeper should be employed for the civil staff, and that on no account should any tribesman be given the work. In the hospitals we have eliminated any post of 'sweeper' and have instead 'medical attendants', all of whom help in cleaning buildings and compounds. When necessary, they and even the doctors themselves empty a bed-pan and this is an excellent example; indeed a hospital is an ideal place to propagate the view that there is nothing derogatory in meeting an elementary human need.

The case of the Assam Rifles is rather different. Some of the jawans are engaged on conservancy work, but they do not usually clean the lavatories, for the Assam Rifles outposts are normally provided with deep-pit latrines.

And this indeed is the real solution of this problem.

I myself lived for twenty years in a tribal village without ever employing a sweeper. We used the pit method and found it quite satisfactory; properly used, with plenty of earth, it does not attract flies and gives off no evil smell. Even now in many parts of the civilized world there are no water-closets and no sweepers; in English villages you will often find the earth-closets.

It will be necessary, however, as the townships grow into towns, to have a few conservancy workers to keep them clean. Such workers should never be asked to clean latrines; they should be quite distinct from 'lavatory-sweepers'; and they should suffer no social disability. We should not employ anyone in NEFA who, on the one hand, would refuse to accept food from the hands of any human being, or on the other hand, from whose hands members of the staff would refuse to eat. Some such rule would act as an automatic check on the introduction of caste prejudices.

We may summarize the ideas of this Chapter in the words of the Prime Minister.

The problem of the tribal areas is to make the people feel that they have perfect freedom to live their own lives and to develop according to their wishes and genius. India to them should signify not only a protecting force but a liberating one. Any conception that India is ruling them and that they are the ruled, or that customs and habits with which they are unfamiliar are going to be imposed upon them, will alienate them and make our frontier problems more difficult.

'We must inspire them with confidence and make them feel at one with India, and realise that they are part of India and have an honoured place in it. This can only be done by allowing them to retain their own cultural traits and habits and leaving them to develop along their own lines without any compulsion from outside.'

Part Seven

CULTURAL AIMS IN NEFA

'A nation needs joy as much as food and knowledge.'

— C. RAJAGOPALACHARI

A Tribal Renaissance

In NEFA we are not aiming at a mere preservation of culture the freezing of social life at its present level. We are striving for a renaissance of art, music, beauty, colour, the joys and graces of living.

Some areas, such as northern Subansiri, have little culture, no art, no dance; life is drab, monotonous, absurd. The Noctes have largely lost their old traditions and now have a dull parody of plains culture. The Sherdukpens are in a state of decay in comparison with the northern Monpas. But other tribal groups are still alive, full of zest for living, with a rare capacity for enjoyment.

The art of tribal people is often greatly affected by the artistic tendency of the surrounding populations. This may be seen very clearly in Manipur where the people of the plains are creative, lovers of the dance, with a strong attraction for colour and an instinct for design. As a result the impact of the Manipuris on such tribes as the Kabuis has been fortunate, for the Kabuis have learnt improvements in technique and a refinement of their original patterns of weaving, and in their dances they have adopted enriching variations from the dances of the plains.

The people of Assam are a beauty-loving and artistic people In an oft-quoted phrase, Mahatma Gandhi once exclaimed that 'the maidens of lovely Assam weave poems on their looms'. No one can with-hold his admiration from the best traditional products of Assamese art, the splendour of its weaving, the grandeur of its temples and the gaiety and variety of its dances. We should expect, therefore, that the tribes living in close proximity to so artistic a people would benefit greatly from the contact.

Unhappily during the later years of the British regime a wave of ugliness passed over the whole of India. In spite of the protests of Rabindranath Tagore and the active opposition of Mahatma Gandhi, vast quantities of cheap foreign cloth poured into the country and the Indian mills were not slow to imitate in colour and design the worst of the foreign models. The old beauty was driven underground and the whole face of the countryside was changed and changed for the worse.

It was not until the coming of Independence that things began to change. Though they are still changing all too slowly, there has been an astonishing renaissance throughout India of the traditional art of the common people. We now have lovely textiles from Rajasthan, Uttar Pradesh, Bombay, Orissa and Bengal. In Assam, efforts have been made to revive the traditional patterns and colours of the old weaving. The art of wood-carving has come again into its own and many beautiful toys and other objects are being made, often by very ordinary folk, throughout India. Work in silver and gold, in cane and bamboo, in clay and in a score of other mediums has been revived. The former beauty had not been killed, it had only been driven underground and one of the most hopeful features of the New India is the way in which people everywhere are turning to the simple and attractive products of the village craftsman, who is thus being encouraged to increase and improve his output.

I have stressed this because it has an important bearing on the art of NEFA. As its people come more and more into contact with the outside world, they are going to be influenced artistically and culturally in many different ways. If the impact on them of civilization is vulgar, shoddy and ugly then that contact will be merely destructive. For it is only natural that the simple peasants from the hills will imitate the products of what they conceive to be a higher civilization. You may see this when any tribesman goes into a shop. His taste, which is so true when dealing with its own products, seems to fail entirely when he comes face to face with manufactured goods and he will often buy the worst coloured and the worst patterned and the least durable object that he sees.

We need to-day in India a William Morris or a Ruskin to lead us in a great crusade against the ugly, the shoddy and the vulgar. In this country, and especially in Assam where artistic values have been held in honour for centuries, this should not really be necessary. But unhappily the prestige of what is foreign has dominated the country far too long and there have been too few people to come forward to guide the public taste.

But to-day there is more than a possibility that side by side with the countrywide renaissance of art we may be approaching a similar renaissance among the tribal people of the hills. There has been a revival of the beautiful and colourful weaving of the Lushais. The folkdance festivals at Delhi and elsewhere have encouraged tribal people all over India to dance more and to dance better. In NEFA too an attempt is being made to revive and develop many of the traditional arts and recreations.

The chief art of NEFA is weaving, which is done exclusively by women using a small tension loom. They belong to a great many different tribes, each of which has its special patterns and colours. In Tuensang and parts of Tirap the stress is on rich reds and blacks and the people here weave shawls, bags, skirts and *lengtis*. Much of this work is of high quality and is very durable. Many of the Adis also are enthusiastic weavers and some of the tribes, such as the Boris, are completely self-sufficient in cloth, making warm and lasting garments mainly of wool. Some of the Adi groups do not weave very much, but the art is rapidly growing among them as yarn is made available and instructors go round the villages to teach and inspire. The Apa Tanis also are expert weavers and we look forward to the day when their products with their charming traditional patterns and bright colours will be as popular in the shops as the Manipuri cloth is to-day.

But to my mind, nothing can compare with the weaving of the Mishmis. This tribe, which in the past has had an undeservedly bad reputation for sloth, is in fact one of the most artistic in the whole of NEFA. The women make excellent coats for their menfolk in a wide variety of styles, which are also bought both by the Adis and by people in the plains. For women they make skirts, blouses and shawls which are quite enchanting. I once brought one of these magnificent shawls of a general maroon colour with silver threads back from tour for my wife and she has often worn it to the admiration of everyone who sees it. The Mishmi bags too are made in a large variety of colour and design and are singularly attractive.

In addition to weaving, some of the NEFA tribes have a tradition of wood-carving. Most of this has a religious or magical basis.

In Kameng bowls, cups and dishes are made; magnificent masks are carved for use in ceremonial dances, and Monpa artists make wooden images of the Lord Buddha. In the Khampti area of Lohit there are wood-carvers who are adept in making beautiful religious images, figures of dancers and other objects. The chief centre of wood-carving, however, is in the Tuensang Division and in the Wancho area of Tirap. Here the wood-carving in the past has been very largely associated with head-hunting and the human head dominates almost everything that is made. Thus you will get many pipes with the bowl carved in the shape of a head; you will get drinking-mugs with warriors carrying off heads in triumph; you will get small wooden heads and little human figures, often done with astonishing realism and power, which again celebrate a successful raid. Some of the tribes also make very good toys for children. It is a problem, now that head-hunting is coming to an end, as to whether this art can survive. But we hope that with proper guidance it will be possible to direct it into other channels.

Another art in which all the tribal people of Assam are expert is work in cane and bamboo wherever these materials are available. Many tribes make their own hats which are often extremely decorative and are adorned with beaks and feathers of birds or with tufts of hair dyed red, and the actual weaving of the cane often reaches a point of the highest efficiency.

Every human being carries in his own body a canvas on which he can exercise his creative imagination. The tribal people who do not (except in Kameng) draw or paint and who are often greatly hampered by the lack of materials for their art, do at least have in their own charming persons an admirable field for self-expression. The ornaments made in the interior of the hills, where they have not been corrupted by cheap plastic articles from the towns, are often ingenious and beautiful. Some tribes make pretty ornaments with the blue wings of birds and the green backs of beetles, or decorate their baskets with the stuffed bodies of bright coloured birds. The Konyaks make a beautiful flower-like ornament for the ear with red seeds and thin slivers of bamboo. All the tribes are very fond of beads and though some just hang strings of them round their necks, others make them into attractive patterns. They also make every sort of head-band and a Konyak girl with her snood of gleaming brass or a Mishmi girl with her crown of bright silver could go anywhere in the world and be admired.

Rightly guided and inspired there is a great future for the art, whether it be music, the dance, weaving, wood-carving, whatever it may be, of the tribal people of NEFA, indeed of the tribal people throughout greater Assam. They have a fresh, original and very precious gift to bring to India. But we must remember that this gift will only be precious so long as it is original. Once tribal art becomes imitative it will quickly lose its value. I am not one of those who would keep tribal art 'as it is' and would discourage change and development. Our approach to everything in life must be creative and dynamic. But equally I am not one of those who believe in trying to improve the art of a people. That seems to me presumptious. In 18th century England various poets attempted to improve Shakespeare and Milton. A 'respectable' version of *The Tempest* was produced with additional characters and *Paradise Lost* was rewritten in heroic couplets. To-day we laugh at those who tried to do good to Shakespeare and Milton, and it may be that those who try to tidy up and refine the music, the dance or the designs of the tribal people may also one day be looked on as ridiculous. The Prime Minister has deprecated attempts to modernize the folk-dance; if this is done, it will lose its charm and splendour. 'Bharat Mata in her various forms must continue to live and prosper.'

Yet this is a serious danger in our training institutions. Youthful instructors from the towns find it hard to follow the policy: 'Improve the technique, but do not spoil the colour and design'. If we are not very careful it may well be that in the course of a few years the fresh beauty of the NEFA textiles will be conventionalized and debased.

For the life of me I cannot see what is wrong with the best tribal designs. Why this passion for 'improving' them? How, in any case, does one *improve* a work of art, and who is to judge whether the change is for the good or not? We do not try to improve the classical designs of India. I fear that it is a subconscious sense of superiority to all things tribal that inspires some of our instructors.

We have, therefore, decided, instead of imposing alien designs from outside, to study Adi or Mishmi or Naga cloth as a whole, and teach the trainess the very best things in their own tradition. Every CITPC has a small collection of textiles which assembles and displays the best products of its area. This not only helps to integrate the institution with the life of the people and increase their pride in their own products, but the teachers then have before them a selection of the best styles to follow.

The control of shops is essential if tribal taste is to be guided. In the past many unsuitable things, even brassieres, falsies and lipstick were imported by the Marwaris and sold to the tribal girls, but the Administration has now issued a directive which aims at eliminating shops owned by outsiders and controlling, so far as is possible, the type of goods brought into NEFA.

Some criticism has been made that this policy attempts to keep the people 'backward' by restricting their access to the products of civilization. We may reply that on the contrary we are making available to them a large range of useful articles and are only opposing these things which will waste their money and spoil their taste. The argument that the new policy means that money will remain in NEFA, and particularly, for example, in the case of cloth, that the money goes into the hands of the women of the tribe instead of into the pocket of a merchant in Calcutta or elsewhere, generally makes a strong appeal. It could also be pointed out that everybody in India lives under some sort of restriction : we cannot buy many 'modern' goods from America. The story of Gandhiji's campaign against foreign goods and mill-cloth might also be told.

Here is an opportunity for NEFA officers to exercise their imagination, their taste, and their intelligence. Let us all try to bring really good things to our people. I will give two examples. In the Kameng Division, very fine fur hats, shoes and coats are sometimes obtained by the tribal people themselves from Kalimpong. These are warm, durable and artistic. We are arranging for our shops to stock them in Kameng and in the colder northern areas of Siang, Subansiri and Lohit.

Then again, in Tirap the people have no shawl or cloak of their own to cover themselves against the cold : they wear white bed-sheets which, quickly becoming dirty, give them a drab and miserable appearance. The shops here, and perhaps also in Tuensang, will stock and sell colourful shawls from the Naga Hills or Manipur, which are in the same general tradition, and these will bring colour to the villages and give inspiration to the handloom industry.

We must remember that many of the NEFA people are better off than their tribal brethren, and even ordinary plains villagers, elsewhere. Some of them are now, in fact, earning quite a lot of money. They can afford to buy good things. They need not be condemned only to the ugly, the shoddy and the cheap. A warm blanket of artistic colour, a good shawl, is well within their means.

In a word, this policy is essentially a positive one and aims at the betterment of the life of the people by providing them with good and useful things; at helping them to save their money; at protecting them from exploitation; at guiding their taste; and at encouraging their own industries and trade.

Art is no mere luxury. Nothing, said the Irish poet W. B. Yeats, is more pleasing to God than 'the glad invention of beautiful and exalted things.' Art is the main-spring of a full and happy life, for he who creates fulfils the purpose for which he was created.

The Revival of Recreations

An important way of countering the sense of inferiority and avoiding detribalization is to revive tribal recreations — dance, song, games. In central India, the dance was at one time dying out completely, for the Gonds and other tribes there got the idea that to dance was not quite respectable and led to their being scorned by their more 'advanced' neighbours. Certain types of missionary also have forbidden their converts to dance or to sing the old songs, permitting them only to sing hymns — or American ragtime. The all-India revival of folk-dancing has already done something to check this tendency, and so has the personal influence of the Prime Minister.

'It is a very great pity' he has said, 'that we in the cities have drifted so far away from the aesthetic side of life. We still have a good many folk-songs and dances when we go to the villages, because modern civilization has more or less left them untouched. The progress of modern civilization in India involves both good things and bad. One of the things we have lost is the spirit of song and dance and the capacity for enjoyment and this is what the tribal people so abundantly have. We seem to pay too much attention to the cinema; it is undoubtedly an excellent medium for many good things, but unfortunately it has not proved to be particularly inspiring. We must imbibe something of the spirit of the tribal folk instead of damping it with our long faces'.

'Tribal culture,' says the Prime Minister again, 'leads to a way of life which particularly makes the people rejoice in song and dance. Our mentors who go to them frown at their ways and tell them to desist from them in the name of reform. The result is that they lose somewhat that joy in life which they possess in abundant measure and gain little else in its place. They become joyless and devitalized, dull and insipid. Surely that is a wrong approach.'

In NEFA the standard of dancing varies greatly from place to place. There is, of course, some very fine dancing. The Tuensang and Tirap tribes can stage a variety of dances, including an exciting war-dance — though with the coming of peace this may not retain its vitality for long. The Monpas and Sherdukpens have remarkable ceremonial pantomimes which the mummers perform with finely-carved and coloured masks. Most of the Adi groups are greatly attached to dancing as a form of recreation, not merely for ceremonial.

But there are other areas where the dance is either severely restricted to ritual occasions or hardly exists as a living art at all. This does not seem to be in any way due to external contact, but to be a very old tradition.

Among the Mishmis, for example, although there are some Idu dances, the Taraons and Kamans dance only for certain rarely performed ceremonies and occasionally in honour of visiting officials. In the Phom, Konyak and Wancho areas I found little spontaneous dancing. These tribes can 'lay on' on a dance for a special occasion such as Republic Day or the visit of a VIP, but it is obvious that the dance is not a part of daily life, as it is among the Adis of Siang or some of the tribes of central India and Bihar. It is rare for girls to dance.

Throughout Subansiri the dance is very poor. The Tagins and Gallongs, as well as the Hill Miris, sometimes perform an uninspired imitation of the classical Adi dance. Some of the Daflas dance a little, but for them too this is not part of the essential tribal culture. In the last three years, however, there has been — under official encouragement — a certain revival cf Apa Tani dancing.

The same may be said of music. Compared with other tribesmen, our's have few musical instruments, their most remarkable deficiency being the lack of the drum. There are Mishmi and Monpa drums, and the Naga groups have great long-drums in their morungs, though the latter are on'y beaten on ceremonial occasions and were mainly associated with head-hunting. The Jews-harp is found and there is a variety of fiddles, but the flute is less commonly used than one would expect. In the main, dances and songs are unaccompanied.

Tribal singing in NEFA makes a very strong appeal to me personally and I have been enchanted by the songs of Konyak and Wancho boys and girls. But even this singing, beautiful as it is, has not much variety. Adi singing has greater liveliness and scope, but in Subansiri, although songs are sung at certain festivals, I found it difficult to persuade the Tagins and Gallongs there to sing at all, and never once heard a spontaneous burst of song, such as delights the ears continually in Siang. The Sherdukpens and Monpas, both men and women, sing but all too often in an uninspired and rather tuneless manner.

There is thus a great deal of room for developing these natural and innocent arts among the people, though it has, of course, to be done with caution. We should be very careful about any attempt to change a dance which is strictly ceremonial into a form of recreation (though this might be done) and should not introduce ritual dances into the educational curriculum, for this might well disturb the orthodox and would probably not succeed.

The task of revival will not be easy, for the drabbest cultural areas are mainly coterminous with the most difficult and drab terrain. But to bring music and colour to these places is almost as important as providing them with food.

What is being done about this?

Touring officers of senior standing are encouraging dances while on tour, and many show a keen and intelligent interest in them; there are dances on all important official occasions. In one Division at least local tribal experts have been invited to the schools, once or twice a week, to teach the children singing and recreational dances; this has the advantage, not only of associating the local tribesmen more closely with the schools, but also of freeing the boys and girls from the temptation, so often present, of regarding their own recreations as beneath them once they become educated.

Many dances have a ceremonial purpose and may not be performed on ordinary occasions. As I have said, this makes the introduction of dancing as part of the school curriculum, sometimes difficult, but there are areas where the dance is recreational in motive and wherever this is so, we are making it part of the school routine. Competitions between schools for the best dancing, tribal dress and ornament, and singing, have been held. Special occasions of jubilation and importance are celebrated by a dance at the school, in which not only the children but the local villagers participate.

An important minor task is to make dancing-grounds, and officers on tour are encouraging the boys and girls to clear and level suitable places in the villages. This has been done with remarkable success in Siang.

The essential thing at the moment is not to improve the dance where it is already flourishing, as, for example, among the Adis, but to revive or introduce it where it does not exist or only exists in a dying or decadent condition.

Where dances are introduced, they should be, as far as possible, of the general cultural area to which they belong. Thus the Idu Mishmis might be encouraged to imitate the Padams, but not the the Sherdukpens or Lushais. The best dances of Tirap or even the Naga Hills might be introduced into Tuensang and vice-versa. We are appointing some of the most expert tribal dancers to go as instructors to areas where the art is unknown.

Dancing-parties might occasionally be taken on visits to culturally impoverished areas. A party of girls from Along might do a lot of good if they danced at Daporijo; a Sherdukpen party of masked dancers visiting Tirap, where the art of wood-carving still exists, might inspire a similar, but typically Naga kind of pantomime there.

I myself have found that the gramophone is generally more appreciated than the radio. The reception is better; it is more practical; and it is possible to replay a popular record. A.I.R. has plans to make gramophone records of NEFA music and whenever possible touring officers should take gramophones and such records with them. Here too it will be advisable to play records of the same general group. Thus I have found Angami records popular in Tirap, where the musical tradition is somewhat similar, but not appreciated at all in Slang. On the other hand, Adi records went down very well indeed in Subansiri. But the radio and gramophone should be used with caution, for there is danger that they may swamp the natural songs of the tribes — Khasi and even more Lushai music is now largely assimilated to the hymn or the cinema-hit — and may make them lazy, so that they will prefer to listen rather than sing themselves.

The people of NEFA have many excellent traditional games — the ant-game and bird-games of the Adis, for example, a rice-husking game (or dance) in Tuensang, the Bobo swinging sport and a snake-game among the Apa Tanis, and the bamboo dance in Tirap. Tribal boys are found of high and low jumping, archery contests, and especially the Tug of War.

The case of the Tug of War illustrates in an interesting way how research is necessary even for so apparently simple a matter as a children's game. The Tug of War cannot be introduced indiscriminately, for in some tribes it has an important ceremonial purpose. The Rengmas use it to divine the future of the crops. If one side is entirely overwhelmed and dragged into another quarter of the village, it foretells death for one of the losing party. Should the creeper break there will be deaths on both sides. In former days, when the creeper was cut, prayers offered that the heads of enemies might be taken. Among the Aos, the Tug of War is, or used to be, associated with certain ceremonies and performed between men and women.

But wherever possible this game might be introduced into the schools, for it is good exercise, great fun and needs no apparatus except a long piece of thick creeper.

The development of a NEFA Theatre, through variety shows and composition of little plays with a local background, is another possibility of great promise.

In NEFA recreation is not a luxury; it is a duty. By making the people happy, it eliminates anxiety and discontent; by filling the time fruitfully, it raises morale. It is an important means, provided it is on the right lines, towards the development of tribal culture. As Kabir says:

> *The hills and the sea and the earth dance;*
> *The world of man dances in laughter and tears.*

The Importance of Research

Accurate information about the people has now been accepted as essential for all proper administration of the tribal areas. As long ago as 1946 the Government of India added a Department of Anthropology to its list of scientific Surveys. Most State Governments which have tribal populations have set up Tribal or Cultural Research institutions. In NEFA too a Department of Research has been established which will in time provide us with information concerning the social life, the mythology and religion, the material culture, the languages and the raciology of NEFA.

The Research Department is not a merely academic Department; we have asked its officers to regard themselves, not so much as anthropologists but as what the great Cambridge scientist Haddon called philanthropologists. Their work, while always trying to maintain the dispassionate ideals of science, is essentially practical. Thus, they will enquire into tribal religion, both to add to the world's knowledge of theology and so that our officers can understand and so respect tribal beliefs. They study material culture so that the information thus obtained may help the development of cottage industries. They examine social and political organization to assist, for example, in the building up of co-operatives on the right lines and to help the development of tribal political institutions. The work of the philologists is not merely academic, but aims at helping officers to learn the tribal languages by providing them with an apparatus of dictionaries and grammars, and at building up a literature for the people based on their own traditions and in their own tongue.

Another valuable way in which the Research staff can help us is by studying tribal taboo and etiquette and thus save us from making fools of ourselves on tour. For example, the Mishmis believe that if anyone sits on the wooden slab which the head of a household uses as a pillow, the latter's expectation of life will be decreased. In some places, to ask an unmarried girl for tobacco is equivalent to an attempt at seduction. No one should ever touch the fence on which the clothes and ornaments of a dead man are hung after his funeral. It is a breach of etiquette to enter any room in a tribal house without warning. All NEFA homes are decorated with the heads of animals taken in the chase or sacrificed at festivals. These make convenient pegs on which to hang a hat or umbrella, but no one should ever do this, for it will bring misfortune to the household.

Officers on tour also have to be very careful about having bamboos cut for camp or even collecting fire-wood from the ground. Certain clumps of bamboo are reserved for ceremonial purposes; certain trees are sacred and even the fallen branches may not be used.

Clyde Kluckhohn has recently given two interesting examples of the value of research in these matters. A poverty-stricken American Indian tribe used to make itself even poorer by destroying the house and property of anyone who died. An anthropologist persuaded the people to cease the practice by an extension of the 'fumigation' procedures already established in their religion. Government's objective was achieved, but 'within the framework of the tribal culture'. The Ashantis of the West Coast of Africa started rebelling against the British Government. It was an anthropologist who discovered the reason: British officials and tourists had been taking back as curios to England certain wooden stools which the people regarded as embodying their guardian spirits.

Even in such a matter as Museums the tribal people are put first. Instead of building up a large Museum in Shillong where it will be a luxury catering to tourists and members of the staff, we are laying the greatest stress on the establishment of Museums in the Divisions. This policy has been followed in Africa, where the display of the finest creations of tribal genius in places readily accessible to the people themselves has greatly encouraged their art. Attached to each Museum there will be an Emporium where local products will be on sale and we hope that when the villagers see their own things not only given place of honour in a Museum, but also purchased by visitors and members of the staff, they will take greater pride, make more of them, and indeed purchase them themselves.

The same policy is being followed with regard to Libraries. Instead of having a large Library in Shillong, we are building up Libraries in the Divisions, which will ultimately, of course, be for the people themselves when they are able to benefit from them. In the meantime, it is regarded as an important thing that our own staff should keep up their reading. It is all too easy in an outpost, or even in a Divisional headquarters, for an officer to grow stale and become indifferent to intellectual pursuits.

On my travels in the interior of NEFA, I have sometimes been a little shocked at the mental apathy of some of our officers. Some boasted that they never opened a newspaper, others that they never read a book. Few have the habit of reading.

The best administrators of tribal people are, generally speaking, men of wide general education, men who read and think. The study of poetry and art enables a man to appreciate many aspects of tribal life. The reading of great fiction enlarges his knowledge of human nature. Any intellectual hobby, the study of botany, of birds and animals, stamp-collecting, photography, and above all, of course, the study of anthropology, psychology and folklore will keep him fresh and help to protect him against the perils of loneliness and the menace of boredom.

Reading, in fact, should have its place in the life of every NEFA officer, and we may remember the example of the great scientist who spent at least half an hour every day of his life in reading poetry so that his spirit would not be overwhelmed by the accumulation of scientific data. Officials should not allow themselves, in the words of Matthew Arnold, to be entirely 'drugged with business'.

CONCLUSION

In this essay I have tried to look at the NEFA Administration from the standpoint of tribal interests and to show how every aspect of its work not only fits together but has its bearing on tribal life.

One of the great achievements of the last three years has been the creation of the Single-Line Administration which stresses the inter-relationship of the entire work and the importance of every aspect of it. Even those members of the staff who do not deal directly with the tribal people have it in their power to influence them, for good or evil. Thus the officers dealing with supply and transport have a vital part to play in maintaining supplies for building institutions and keeping the staff supplied with the necessities of life. But equally they have the opportunity of ensuring that the goods imported into NEFA will not corrupt tribal taste or tempt the people to waste their money on unnecessary and unsuitable things, but will rather enrich their life with the best products (within, of course, a limited price-range) that India, traditionally an artistic and beauty-loving country, can supply.

The Assam Rifles can play a large part, not only in maintaining law and order, but in setting an example to the people of smartness, discipline, self-help and the dignity of maunal labour. By their friendliness and readiness to help in all emergencies, the jawans have always proved good ambassadors and their influence has been of great value in integrating the people with the rest of India. And indeed, but for the demands of the recent crisis in the Naga Hills, they would have been even more closely associated with the development programme, in the making of roads and bridges, and in the growing of food.

The work and influence of the office assistant, the accountant or the Sub-Treasury Officer is not confined to the keeping of accounts and dealing with files. The people of NEFA are remarkably sensitive to two things: the first is delay, the second is corruption. The prompt and courteous settlement of bills, whether for contracts, porterage, casual labour on roads, air-strips or buildings; a readiness to spare time to listen to a grievance; the elimination of long waits outside an office — have their social and political effect. And conversely, delay, neglect, irritability. and impatience create the worst possible impression on the tribal mind and foster the sense of inferiority and alienness.

Integrity, fidelity in the keeping of accounts, a constant watch to see that Government money is put to the best possible use for the benefit of the people, the determination that the bulk of the money will be spent for their good and not for the staff are of the utmost value in winning the sometimes suspicious and critical heart of the educated tribesman.

Even the motor-driver, the peon, the medical attendant in the hospital has his part to play in this great task. The tribal people look at the Administration as a whole, and however good a Political Officer may be himself, he will fail unless he can inspire his entire staff with his own ideals. One bad assistant, or corrupt chaprassi, or oppressive interpreter can undo much of the good done by the higher officers.

Success in the very delicate task of steering a middle way between leaving too much alone and interfering too officiously and imposing too heavily on the life of the people will depend on an appreciation of the fundamental ideas set out by the Prime Minister. As an aid to this, we might well adopt the following touchstones for any scheme for development, welfare, relief and expansion: the sentences within quotation marks are from the Prime Minister's own speeches and notings.

1. Will the scheme help the tribesmen 'to grow according their own genius and tradition'?
2. Or will its result be merely 'to shape them according to our own image or likeness and impose on them our particular way of living'?
3. Will it tend to make of the tribesmen 'a second-rate copy of ourselves'?
4. Will it 'uproot the tribal people from their surroundings' and 'make them grow soft and thus lose some of their fine qualities' ?
5. It is open to the criticism that 'it is grossly presumptious on our part to approach the tribesmen' with an air of superiority or to tell them what to do or not to do' ?
6. Will it involve too rapid a process of acculturation or, in other words, are we trying to go too fast ?

7. Is there any danger that we are overwhelming the tribes by too many projects, each good in itself, but in the aggregate imposing too heavy a burden ?
8. Will it impair or destroy in any way the self-reliance of the people ?
9. Is it really, on a long-term basis, for the ultimate good of the tribesmen, or is it simply something that will make a good show in the press or an official report ?
10. Will it help to integrate the tribal people with Greater Assam and with India as a whole ?

NEFA offers a unique opportunity to every member of the Administration, for the task it is attempting is probably unique in the history of civilization's dealings with primitive people. Elsewhere in the world, colonists have gone into tribal areas for what they can get; the Government of India has gone into NEFA for what it can give. Whenever a new project is considered or policy proposed, the one criterion is whether it will be for the benefit of the tribal people.

The keynote of the Administration's policy indeed is this : the tribesmen first, the tribesmen last, the tribesmen all the time.

During the last three years, astonishing progress has been made. The entire Administration has been recognized, high standards of efficiency and integrity have been established, the many divergent interests and plans have been integrated. A tradition has already grown up and more and more officers have had their imagination captured by what I have described as the Philosophy of NEFA.

The difficulties have been almost overwhelming and only a united, enthusiastic team sincerely devoted to a high ideal could have met them unafraid. Problems of movement and supply, lack of trained personnel, the difficult terrain, persistent if uninformed criticism from outside, the constant threat of political infection from the disturbed areas so near at hand, have made still more exacting a task which would have been formidable under the most favourable conditions.

There is no complacency in the NEFA Administration and its own officers are its severest critics. It has still a long way to go, both in practical achievement and in the full implementation of the scientific and humanitarian ideals which inspire it. But a start has been made and it is on the way.

The tribal people of NEFA offer us a very special challenge. Their simplicity, which is most lovable; their art, which often gives them the dignity of princes but is so easily destroyed; their courtesy and hospitality, discipline and self-reliance; their ability to work hard and co-operatively; their occasional bewilderment before the advance of an unfamiliar world, and yet their welcome and friendliness to that world; these things win the heart and call for the very best in those who try to serve them. Nothing can be too good for them, but with what care that good has to be shared!